THE TRANSFORMED HEART

Daily Encounters with a Transformational God

by

Michael D. Warden

Ascent Books & Media
an imprint of the Ascent Coaching Group Inc.

The Transformed Heart
Copyright © 2008 Michael Warden

Published by Ascent Books & Media, an imprint of the Ascent Coaching Group Inc., 9901 Brodie Lane Suite 160, Austin, Texas 78748. www.ascentcoachinggroup.com

ISBN 978-0-6152-0556-4

Printed in the United States of America

DEDICATION

To all those of noble heart
who refuse to settle for less
than God's highest dream for their lives

INTRODUCTION

IT'S a Big Life you're called to lead. There's a Big Dream in your heart, placed there by God himself. You know it's there, even though, like most of us, you lose track of it from time to time. It bubbles up in you, though, most every day. It comes upon you as a persistent desire for *something more* out of life. A desire to *do* something more. A desire to *be* something more. You know, deep down, that there's got to be more to your life than this. It's like you're being summoned to a Higher Purpose, and a Bigger Life.

Because, in fact, you are.

But there's a difficult truth we have to face. Living a Big Life is hard. It takes work and sacrifice, and most of all, a lot of faith. Leading a small life is far easier and more comfortable. However ultimately dissatisfying, a small, cozy, ordinary life is far less threatening. To die from a slow painless bleed seems better on the surface than to perish in the manner of a hero like William Wallace in the movie *BraveHeart*.

But then, no one around us would be set free.

The real question is this: On what will you spend your life? For it will surely be spent on something, whether consciously chosen or not. If you must spend it, why not then spend it for something as big and meaningful as God's big dream for you? To spend it on your own comfort or glory is the height of egocentricity. To spend it on trying to keep your heart "safe" is wholly insane. As Helen Keller so rightly pointed out, "Life is either a daring adventure or nothing. Security does not exist in nature, nor do the children of men as a whole experience it. Avoiding danger is no safer in the long run than exposure."

To choose the greater way—not the way of safety or comfort—is to abandon your life to a Greater Power and a Greater Purpose. It is to dive headlong into the rapids, knowing full well that in the moment you do, you relinquish your right to choose your own course. The ride through this world is no longer yours. Your job now is simply to stay in the main flow of the current, to enjoy the thrill and glory of the ride and the beauty of the surroundings. And to laugh for the joy you have found in surrendering your life to a Higher Call.

Isn't that the life you've always wanted, anyway? Of course it is. Because it is precisely the life you were designed to live.

The Transformed Heart devotional is your personal guide to experiencing that bigger life. Covering a period of six months, the weekday readings invite you to connect with Christ through his Word on a truly intimate, relational level—by learning to notice where God is already actively at work in your heart and life, and intentionally partnering with him in a way that leads to authentic life transformation.

To assist in this good work, each devotion includes not only scripture and a devotional reading, but also an interactive, challenging action step that is designed to inspire you toward God's heart and purpose for your life in practical, meaningful ways. To get the most from this journey, it's important that you do your best to complete all the action steps, even those that may take little extra time. You'll find the extra effort will be well worth the cost.

Weekends on this journey are reserved for reflection—to solidify what you've learned during the week and intentionally apply it to your life in meaningful ways. For that reason, instead of devotional readings, the weekend portions of the devotional include a guide for reflection and application. To maximize your benefit, I suggest you take time on Saturday morning to go through the Weekend Reflection questions, then continue to ponder and journal your responses to those questions throughout the weekend.

Your big life in Christ is waiting to be revealed. So take heart, and hold on to your courage. Jesus loves you, and he is with you right now. Let the journey begin.

Note: For information on other resources related to *The Transformed Heart*, or to learn more about the author's life and work, please visit www.ascentcoachinggroup.com.

WHERE YOU ARE NOW
Week 1—Monday

I am the gate; whoever enters through me will be saved.
He will come in and go out, and find pasture.
The thief comes only to steal and kill and destroy;
I have come that they may have life, and have it to the full.
(John 10:9-10)

LET'S begin with a question: How satisfied are you with your life right now? I realize that can be a tough question to answer off the top of your head. So here's a simple tool I'd like you to use right now to find out. Next to each life category below, rate your current level of satisfaction in that area from 1 to 10—10 being "absolutely satisfied in every way."

Category	Level of Satisfaction
Career	
Money/Finances	
Personal/Spiritual Growth	
Health/Fitness	
Fun & Recreation	
Friends	
Family	
Significant Other/Romance	
Contribution/Service (making an impact on your community & the world)	
Where You Live (your home, city, region of the world)	

How'd you do? Now let me ask another question: If you really had "life to the full," what would it look like?

Now wait. Don't just breeze past the question and keep reading—stop a moment and really think about it. If your life truly was abundant and full in *every* way, in *every* arena of your life, in *every* relationship, what would it look like?

For example, where would you live? Who would be with you? What would be your career or ministry? How would you spend your free time? What sorts of things would you find yourself saying about your life? What would other people say about you? What impact would you be making on the world?

Most of us never ask ourselves questions like that. We're too busy wrestling with the monotonous dragons of work and responsibility we face every day, or frantically trying to clear out the rubble-filled path of tasks and to-dos ahead of us—if only to make the walk a little easier for a day or two. We don't have time to think about what a truly abundant life would entail for us. Besides, we realize, doing so would probably only bring us down.

But there's a deeper reason many of us rarely dream about what a life of true abundance would be like for us. Somewhere inside, we're afraid that if we allow ourselves to dream along those lines, we may have to confront how little we actually believe that what Jesus said is true: "I have come that they may have life, and have it to the full" (John 10:10).

MAKE IT REAL!

Copy the results of the Satisfaction Test into your personal journal. Then, in each of the categories, write out a description of what a truly abundant and fulfilling life would look like in that arena. For example, what would it look like to have real abundance and fulfillment in your friendships? What kind of friends would you surround yourself with? What kind of friend would you be? What kinds of things would you do together? Do this for *every* category. Then take the descriptions you've created to God, and lay them brazenly out before him. Invite him to take you into your deepest heart, and father you toward the fulfillment of his highest dream for "life to the full" in you.

FINDING YOUR TRUE SELF IN GOD
Week 1—Tuesday

Surely you desire truth in the inner parts;
you teach me wisdom in the inmost place.
(Psalm 51:6)

IN his book, *Waking the Dead,* John Eldredge writes, "[Jesus] wants truth in the inmost being, and to get it there he's got to take us into our inmost being." But what does it mean to go into your inmost being? The Hebrew word for "inmost being" refers to our deepest thoughts and desires, the core of who we are. In other words, it's talking about our *hearts*. For Jesus to get his transforming truth into our inmost being, he needs us to take a journey into our hearts—and let him show us what's really there.

If you are frightened by the prospect of going into your deepest heart—don't be. For the heart is the place where Jesus dwells; it is his home in you. It's the place he meets with you, and you with him. And he has planted treasures there he's waiting for you to find—visions and longings of the life he meant you to have, which—contrary to what you may been taught—is precisely the life you really always wanted. "Life to the full" isn't about self-worship or creating a life that serves your flesh. It's about becoming all that you were meant to be, being *fulfilled* in that regard, and bringing that gift to the world.

To choose this path, to actually lay plans to pursue the life of abundance Christ meant you to have, is a brave decision. It means breaking rules and busting through barriers that may have become quite familiar and even cozy because of the illusion of safety they convey. It means surrendering your control to a Power and a Will greater than yourself—and letting him carry you to the very place you always wanted to go. "If you cling to your life, you will lose it; but if you give it up for me, you will find it" (Matthew 10:39, NLT).

That's one reason the choice to live a fulfilling life in Christ is a radical act. We all live in a world that favors the mundane, the ordinary, the "just be like everybody else." There will be a cost to going after "life to the full" in God. (They murdered Jesus because of it, if you'll recall.) But at the end of the road, when you finally appear before the throne of God, you will be able to say with genuine joy that you lived well in Christ; that you went after the dreams he planted in your heart, and that you fulfilled your purpose in exactly the way you were meant to.

Justice Oliver Wendall Holmes once said, "Too many people die with their music still in them." Committing your heart to pursue "life to the full" in Christ grants you the stage where you can finally let loose your own special song and dance in the special way that God made you to dance—a way that no one else has ever seen, or could ever do.

MAKE IT REAL!

When Christians talk about the "heart," they often think they're simply talking about emotions. But the Bible describes the heart as much more than just your feelings. To learn more about what your heart really is, do a study on the word *heart* in scripture. Using a concordance or Bible software program, look up every reference to *heart* or *hearts* in both the Old and New Testament. Examine the way the word is used in context, and take note of all the qualities the "heart" refers to within us. Be warned! Doing this will likely transform your relationship with God—and with yourself.

FORGIVEN
Week 1—Wednesday

He made Him who knew no sin to be sin on our behalf, so that we might become the righteousness of God in Him.
(2 Corinthians 5:21, NASB)

WHEN I was a child, I used to dream about Christmas all year long. Early in the year I would begin compiling a list of the gifts I most wanted to receive. As the months went by, I would add to it new things, take away old things I no longer cared to have, and meticulously arrange the items in order of desire. I was careful to keep the list to myself until I was certain I had it just right, then I'd spring it on my mom, usually sometime in October, to make sure she had plenty of time to do my bidding. Of course, I rarely got all that I asked for. But I still savored with joy the anticipation of it all. During the final week leading up to Christmas morning, I would often spread out a sleeping bag on the floor next to the tree, and fall asleep to the blinking of the lights and my own dreams of all the fun I would have come Christmas afternoon.

In those days, I didn't really grasp all that Christmas meant—what it really stood for, or why we celebrated it. But I did understand that it was about receiving wonderful gifts. And it's still about that today.

I think Christians struggle so profoundly with genuinely receiving God's gift of forgiveness and forgiving ourselves because we do not understand the true essence of the gift that Jesus brought to us by coming to earth. Through Christ's death and resurrection, God did something far more than merely take away the punishment your sin deserves.

He gave you an entirely new heart.

MAKE IT REAL!

In your journal, write your response to these questions: What do you really believe about your own heart as a Christ-follower? What assumptions do you have about your heart? In what ways are you suspicious of it? What judgments do you hold against it? How much do you trust it? And finally, how do all of those responses line up against what scripture says is true about your new heart in Christ?

WHO YOU ARE NOW
Week 1—Thursday

But God, being rich in mercy, because of His great love with which He loved us, even when we were dead in our transgressions, made us alive together with Christ (by grace you have been saved), and raised us up with Him, and seated us with Him in the heavenly places in Christ Jesus, so that in the ages to come He might show the surpassing riches of His grace in kindness toward us in Christ Jesus. For by grace you have been saved through faith; and that not of yourselves, it is the gift of God; not as a result of works, so that no one may boast.
(Ephesians 2:4-9, NASB)

THROUGH Christ's death and resurrection, you have been reborn with an entirely new identity through Christ. As Paul explains in Ephesians 2:4-9, through grace, your spirit which was dead, has been made alive in Christ. You have been raised up with Christ and seated with him as a co-heir in God's eternal kingdom. This is an accomplished work. It is finished. And it is a gift, received through the act of authentically placing your faith in Christ (Romans 4:22-24).

As a result of this miraculous rebirth, you exist today in a perpetual state of grace under God. You live each day in a state of forgiveness. You are no longer subject to condemnation because you have already been approved by God (Romans 8:1-2). Yes, you were once far from him, but by the blood of Christ, you have been brought near (Ephesians 2:13). You have been adopted as his beloved child (Romans 8:15). From the moment that happened, you have been his. And no person, no power, no act in all creation can ever snatch you away from his hand.

That is the fundamental gift of salvation—the regeneration of your spirit from death to life in absolute union with God.

It is, truly, an amazing gift. And it is only the beginning.

MAKE IT REAL!

Gather your responses to yesterday's "Make It Real!" questions, and share them with a trusted Christian ally. Hold nothing back. Then ask him or her to pray with you for God's grace to let go of any and all lies you have believed about your heart, and embrace the fullness of God's truth regarding who you really are as a child of the King.

A JOURNEY OF RECLAIMING
Week 1—Friday

Now may the God of peace Himself sanctify you entirely; and
may your spirit and soul and body be preserved complete,
without blame at the coming of our Lord Jesus Christ. Faithful is
He who calls you, and He also will bring it to pass.
(1 Thessalonians 5:23-24, NASB)

IF you have come into a personal, ongoing relationship with
Christ, then you are in the middle of a journey of radical
transformation. Indeed, in the most fundamental way, you have
already been changed. You have been made new; you are reborn.
Your spirit—the eternal living core of who you really are—has
been sprinkled with the blood of Christ, and through his
forgiveness has been declared righteous. And that same spirit has
been sealed in an unshakeable union with the Holy Spirit of God
(Ephesians 1:13-14).

This regeneration of your spirit has fundamentally
transformed the core of who you are, and set you on a journey of
transforming and sanctifying all the other aspects of your
identity—your thoughts, your will, and your emotions. This
amazing state of grace has been granted to you because God
loves you and is passionate about empowering you to become all
that he originally intended. Without the gift of his forgiveness
and grace, you will never become all you were meant to be. But
now that you have received his magnificent gift, nothing can stop
you from achieving that goal.

Nothing, that is, except your own unbelief.

MAKE IT REAL!

When God looks at you, he sees a beautiful soul reborn; a
precious spirit set free, endowed with splendor and grace; a son
or daughter who is absolutely, irreversibly, the apple of his eye.
In your journal, ponder this: What if God is right about you?
What then?

TAKE a few moments this weekend to review the devotions you've read over this past week, as well as the "Make It Real!" steps you've done. As you reflect on the week, get curious about how God is moving in and through your life. Use these questions as a guide:

- ❖ What insights have you gained over the past week?
- ❖ What changes or shifts are you noticing in your relationship with God? with others? with yourself?
- ❖ What "Make It Real!" steps were the most meaningful for you? What made them meaningful?
- ❖ How will you live differently next week as a result of what you've learned?
- ❖ What support do you need to help you make that change?
- ❖ Based on your experiences over the past week, what do you most need from God right now?
- ❖ What do you suppose God might be wanting most from you right now?

CHALLENGE: If you missed one of the "Make It Real!" steps for this week, set aside time this weekend to complete it, and record your reactions, insights, and results in your journal.

A JOURNEY IN THE LIGHT
Week 2—Monday

*But if we walk in the Light as He Himself is in the Light, we have
fellowship with one another, and the blood of Jesus His Son
cleanses us from all sin. If we say that we have no sin, we are
deceiving ourselves and the truth is not in us. If we confess our
sins, He is faithful and righteous to forgive us our sins and to
cleanse us from all unrighteousness.*
(1 John 1:7-9)

BECAUSE of the gift of salvation in Christ, at your core you
are no longer who you once were. You are different. You are a
new creation. Still, though we are fully accepted by God and free
from condemnation, our salvation is not yet complete. There is
still an "old nature" within us, a nature that continues to resist
God's love and submission to his lordship in our lives. We are all
intimately familiar with this old nature, and often tend to define
ourselves by it—as if the old nature were, in fact, our "true self,"
and that our new identity in Christ were some kind of idealized
movie character role we are called to play as best we can. But as
Paul explains in Romans 7:15-23, that old nature does not reside
in your spirit or "inner being" (as Paul refers to it), but in your
body itself (which is why the old nature is often referred to as
"the flesh"). The old nature is not who you are now—for you
have been made new in Christ—rather, it exists within you as the
lingering vestiges of who you were without Christ.

So then, the second phase of God's great gift—that is, the
sanctification of your soul—is essentially this: partnering with
the Holy Spirit to identify and subdue the remnants of the old
nature within you so that the core of your true self in Christ is set
free to live and follow God unhindered in the world.

The Apostle John called this "walking in the Light." When
you stray from the Path, no blatant theatrics are needed to
convince God you're sorry. No self-condemnation or self-abuse
is required to pay for your error. Just repent, get back on the Path,
and continue on with Christ. By practicing this process as a
spiritual discipline, you will stay connected to the wonderful gift

of God's forgiveness and grace, and assure that your fellowship with him and with others will remain strong.

MAKE IT REAL!

Draw a line down the middle of a sheet of paper. Title the left side "My True Self in Christ," and the right side "My Old Nature." Under each heading, list the character traits or behaviors that you think define each one. Notice where you are unsure of what to write, or have trouble coming up with ideas. Complete your lists by going through the New Testament, beginning in the book of Romans, and looking for specific attributes or qualities that scripture identifies with the "flesh" or to your new nature in Christ.

THE GRACE-DRIVEN LIFE
Week 2—Tuesday

But because of his great love for us, God, who is rich in mercy, made us alive with Christ even when we were dead in transgressions—it is by grace you have been saved. And God raised us up with Christ and seated us with him in the heavenly realms in Christ Jesus, in order that in the coming ages he might show the incomparable riches of his grace, expressed in his kindness to us in Christ Jesus. For it is by grace you have been saved, through faith—and this not from yourselves, it is the gift of God—not by works, so that no one can boast. For we are God's workmanship, created in Christ Jesus to do good works, which God prepared in advance for us to do.
(Ephesians 2:4-10)

FOR the Christian—indeed, for every human on earth—grace is everything. Grace is the secret of a heart set free. Grace is the power to become everything you were meant to be. It is the ability to overcome any obstacle, or to stand unmoved against any attack. It is divine power—holy, righteous, pure, and unbreakable…greater than any sin or any enemy. Grace is God's love expressed. It is to the follower of Christ what air is to the wings of an eagle, or wind to the taut sails of a schooner on the open sea.

Grace is utterly beautiful. And utterly free. Perhaps, for so many of us, that's also why it is so hard to accept as real, and surrender to it.

But only those who are willing to accept it—free and without conditions—will ever understand what it really means to follow God, or grasp just how much the love of God is willing to risk for the chance to win your heart.

MAKE IT REAL!

In your journal, create a timeline that describes your own personal history of experience with God's grace. When did you first notice God's grace showing up in your life? What happened? What other times in your history has God's grace played an integral role? What about the times when grace seemed absent? What do you think was really going on during those times?

WHAT IS GRACE, ANYWAY?
Week 2—Wednesday

Therefore, since we have been justified through faith, we have peace with God through our Lord Jesus Christ, through whom we have gained access by faith into the this grace in which we now stand. And we rejoice in the hope of the glory of God.
(Romans 5:1-2)

ALL of my life, I have heard *grace* defined as "God's unmerited favor," which is, of course, true as far it goes. But "God's unmerited favor" is such a vague and frustrating description of something so crucial to the Christian journey. After all, you could rightly say that God's love, God's mercy, and God's kindness could all be defined as "God's unmerited favor." What, then, distinguishes grace from these?

Author and theologian Dallas Willard defines *grace* as "God acting in our life to accomplish what we cannot do on our own." That comes much closer to something I can grab hold of, but even it leaves me a bit unsatisfied. It still feels too far removed from me—something God is up to over there, off in the distance. How do I *intimately live* in such a grace, and build my life upon it in any practical way?

I think the reason we struggle to define *grace* is because it is so radically foreign to the way we would do things if we were God. To our human sensibilities, God's grace seems ridiculously reckless and unwise. How foolish to irrevocably proclaim someone as acceptable and worthy of love and honor and to promise them your full, permanent support before they've actually proven themselves to be the slightest bit worthy of any of these things. Such a gift could be easily abused. It could be taken for granted. It could be horribly wasted. Surely God is too smart for that.

But such is the daring love and wisdom of God. For grace is just such a radical gift. And it takes a radical faith to grab hold of it.

MAKE IT REAL!

Get together with a trusted Christian ally and talk about the role of God's grace in each of your lives. How do you each define *grace?* What do you really believe about grace? What practical impact does grace actually have on your daily experience? How do you receive grace? How do you stay connected to it? What needs to happen for you both to grow in grace?

THE TWO SIDES OF GRACE
Week 2—Thursday

For if, by the trespass of the one man, death reigned through that one man, how much more will those who receive God's abundant provision of grace and of the gift of righteousness reign in life through the one man, Jesus Christ.
(Romans 5:17)

GOD'S grace is two-fold. It is first God's absolute acceptance and approval of who you are, *just as you are*—based solely upon your expressed faith in the redemptive gift of his Son. Once you step into faith, and receive the gift of Christ, you no longer have anything else you need to prove or anywhere else you need to go or anything else you need to do to make yourself right enough or good enough or acceptable enough. You are already *good*—completely acceptable and approved. The God of the universe has proclaimed you as such. What higher court is there?

But if that weren't ridiculously radical enough, grace goes farther even than this. For beyond the grace of absolute acceptance just as you are, grace is also the power to become all that you were meant to be. To tweak Dallas Willard's definition, grace is God's power working *within us and through us* to accomplish what we could never do on our own. Such grace is not fueled by guilt or shame or the rules of religion, but rather through believing that what God has proclaimed concerning you is actually, really true. As a wise man once said, "Show me a man who tries to become righteous by doing righteous things, and I will show you a slave of religion. But show me a man who does righteous things because God has proclaimed him righteous, and I will show you a son of God."

Grace is the power to love sacrificially, the power to walk in intimate communion with God, the power to accomplish God's purpose in the world, the power to overcome any sin, the power to become in every way the whole person you were created to be. And we plug into that life-changing power through our faith—that is, through our confident belief that all of these things are not only possible for us; they are ours by right as sons and daughters of God.

MAKE IT REAL!

What does it mean to you to "reign" in life? On a scale of 1 to 10, how would you say you are doing when it comes to "reigning" in your own life? If you scored yourself less than a 10, take some time to read and meditate on Romans 5–8. As you read, ask yourself, "What part of this am I missing in my own life?" Then ask God to show you the way to fill in the gaps in your understanding and experience of his grace.

THE PROCESS OF FREEDOM
Week 2—Friday

Therefore, there is now no condemnation for those who are in Christ Jesus, because through Christ Jesus the law of the Spirit of life set me free from the law of sin and death.
(Romans 8:1-2)

TO live in God's grace *is* to live in freedom. But too often, somehow we don't feel all that free. We fall short of grace. Honestly, we don't know what the problem is. Yes, we know God loves and accepts us. Yes, his power is available to help us. But it's not enough. For some reason, grace doesn't work for us. It doesn't quite reach us.

Why is that? Perhaps because deep down, we don't really believe that God is right. Sure, he sees us as acceptable and worthy and capable of becoming all we were meant to be. But we know better. So long as we hold onto that sort of subtle arrogance, grace will remain out of reach. As the scripture says, "God is opposed to the proud, but gives grace to the humble" (James 4:6 NASB).

It isn't enough to simply believe that *God* sees you as acceptable, or that *God* believes you can become all that he intended you to be. *You must see yourself that way as well.* You must let go of your own appraisal of your worth and allow God's grace to extend *inward*—into the way you see and deal with your own heart.

You see, when God proclaims you as acceptable and empowered, he's not just rattling off his opinion. He is pronouncing what is actually true. In fact, his very pronouncement *makes* it true, for his creative power rests in his words (Genesis 1).

When you walk in this inner grace of accepting and loving yourself in the way God accepts and loves you, you can finally give yourself permission to be where you are right now in your own journey, without any judgment or condemnation. You can let yourself feel what you are feeling, stumble where you are stumbling, and not know what you are unsure of—all without judging yourself unworthy or less than acceptable to God, yourself, or anyone else. And through it all, you can know that tomorrow you will be closer to the person God created you to be than you are today—because you are actively cooperating with his power, which is actively at work in you, transforming you inevitably into the image of Christ (1 Corinthians 15:10).

That is grace. Utterly beautiful. And utterly true.

MAKE IT REAL!

How are you at loving and accepting yourself just as you are—the same way God loves and accepts you? If you are in conflict over this, recognize that resistance as pride, and confess it to a trusted Christian ally or spiritual mentor. Repent and ask God for the grace to absolutely and completely accept as true what he has proclaimed is true about you.

WEEKEND REFLECTION

TAKE a few moments this weekend to review the devotions you've read over this past week, as well as the "Make It Real!" steps you've done. As you reflect on the week, get curious about how God is moving in and through your life. Use these questions as a guide:

- ❖ What insights have you gained over the past week?
- ❖ What changes or shifts are you noticing in your relationship with God? with others? with yourself?
- ❖ What "Make It Real!" steps were the most meaningful for you? What made them meaningful?
- ❖ How will you live differently next week as a result of what you've learned?
- ❖ What support do you need to help you make that change?
- ❖ Based on your experiences over the past week, what do you most need from God right now?
- ❖ What do you suppose God might be wanting most from you right now?

CHALLENGE: If you missed one of the "Make It Real!" steps for this week, set aside time this weekend to complete it, and record your reactions, insights, and results in your journal.

YOUR ROLE IN GOD'S STORY
Week 3—Monday

You are looking only on the surface of things. If anyone is confident that he belongs to Christ, he should consider again that we belong to Christ just as much as he. For even if I boast somewhat freely about the authority the Lord gave us for building you up rather than pulling you down, I will not be ashamed of it.
(2 Corinthians 10:7-8)

RIGHT at this moment, God is in the middle of telling a grand and powerful Story in the world. He has been telling this Story since the beginning of time, and its plot will continue to unfold until the day Jesus returns. It is a Story about God's passionate desire for intimate communion with all people everywhere throughout time, about the brokenness in humanity that has severed our hope for the communion he desires, and the power of his love to redeem and restore our hearts back to abundant life and intimacy with him.

For much of my life, I have been ashamed of the role God has called me to play in the Story he is telling. Like Moses on Mount Sinai, I have put God off, stammering on about this reason or that why I could not possibility take up the role he wanted me to play. It was too dangerous; too unlike me, I thought. I looked on the role with disdain and suspicion. Clearly, I believed, he had the wrong guy.

Every follower of Christ has a part in the Story he is telling in the world. It is a part unique to you, and you alone have been granted the authority and the privilege to carry it out. God has never chosen the wrong role for any of his children. You are perfect for the part he has called you to play. And the authority to play it has already been granted to you.

But you will never play it fully—or perhaps at all—until you surrender your doubt about yourself or the role, and accept the authority God has granted you to play it.

MAKE IT REAL!

What is the role God is calling you to play in the world? If you aren't certain, try this: In your journal, write a description of the role (or life purpose) you *suspect* God may be calling you to fulfill. Afterward, write a description of the role *you would love to play* in the grand Story God is telling in the world. Notice the similarities and differences in the two descriptions, and ask God to bring clarity to his vision for your life.

SURRENDERING YOUR TREASURE
Week 3—Tuesday

Then the Lord said to him, "What is that in your hand?"
"A staff," he replied.
The Lord said, "Throw it on the ground."
Moses threw it on the ground and it became a snake, and he ran
from it. Then the Lord said to him, "Reach out your hand and
take it by the tail." So Moses reached out and took hold of the
snake and it turned back into a staff in his hand...So Moses took
his wife and sons, put them on a donkey and started back to
Egypt. And he took the staff of God in his hand.
(Exodus 4:2-4, 20)

THERE is always something you must surrender before you can
take up with authority the role God is calling you to play in the
world. The thing you must surrender is a little different for
everyone, but is always something you treasure—something that
you believe defines you or keeps you safe. Perhaps it is your
dream for riches, for a particular kind of career, for marriage, or
for health. Or perhaps it is something less tangible, such as your
dream to be admired or respected, to be safe, or known as
sensible and smart.

It is only when you throw it down that you see your treasure
for the snake—that is, the *deception*—that it is. Remember the
parable of the pearl of great price (Matthew 13:45-46)? The role
you are called to play in God's Story is bigger, more lovely, and
more valuable by far than any lesser "treasure" you have placed
your hope in until now. But only when you let it go will you see
it.

But God, rather than abolishing the thing you throw down,
redeems it. He takes ownership of your surrendered treasure, and
makes it into something new, weaving it into the role he calls you
to play. Moses probably knew from early on that God had called
him to play a significant role in the story of Israel's redemption.
But he could not take up the role until he surrendered his treasure
to God. Who knows what Moses relinquished the day he threw
down his staff? His safety? His desire to be respected? His trust

in his own strength? Whatever it was, he remained a shepherd of sheep until the day he surrendered his staff to God, and became God's shepherd to a nation.

MAKE IT REAL!

What is it that you resist surrendering to God? Make a list, then share it with one or two of your closest Christian allies. Ask them to join you in praying for the faith to surrender these "treasures" to God so that you can wholeheartedly say yes to his call on your life.

*After the death of Moses the servant of the Lord, the Lord said to
Joshua son of Nun, Moses' aide: "Moses my servant is dead.
Now then, you and all these people, get ready to cross the Jordan
River into the land I am about to give to them...Be strong and
courageous, because you will lead these people to inherit the
land I swore to their forefathers to give them. Be strong and very
courageous. Be careful to obey all the law my servant Moses
gave you; do not turn from it to the right or to the left, that you
may be successful wherever you go...Have I not commanded
you? Be strong and courageous. Do not be terrified; do not be
discouraged, for the Lord your God will be with you wherever
you go."*
(Joshua 1:1-2, 6-7, 9)

IT takes extraordinary courage to say yes to your role in God's
grand Story. The simple reason for this is that the role he calls
you to is always bigger than you are. It is always well beyond
your natural ability to accomplish. With every fiber of your
being, you know that you cannot do it. You are clearly incapable.
And yet, because it is God who calls, you say yes. You accept
your role in the Story.

Now that is courage! But notice from where it springs. "Have
I not commanded you?" says God. "Am I not the Lord? Am I not
the Ruler of all the universe? Am I not the Source of all wisdom
and knowledge, of all power and glory and truth? I Am. And I
say that you are the one I choose for this role. You, and not
someone else. Take it! Take up the role with courage and
authority. Have I not commanded you?"

The success of the role God calls you to is not dependent on
your ability, but God's. By commanding Joshua to fulfill the role
of Israel's leader, God imparted to him his own authority and
power to see the task accomplished just as he designed. Joshua's
only true part in the story was to believe, surrender, and obey.
Without that surrendering faith, Joshua would never have found

the courage to say yes to the great role God called him to play. And without that same faith, neither will you.

What would it look like if you really had "surrendering faith" around the role the God is calling you to play in his Grand Story? What would change about the way you live? What would you finally let go of? What would you grab hold of with all your heart? Write a description of your life as you imagine it would be if you fully surrendered to the role God is calling you to play.

Such confidence as this is ours through Christ before God. Not that we are competent in ourselves to claim anything for ourselves, but our competence comes from God. He has made us competent as ministers of a new covenant—not of the letter but of the Spirit; for the letter kills, but the Spirit gives life.
(2 Corinthians 3:4-6)

ONCE you have surrendered your treasure to God and accepted the call to fulfill your unique role in his grand Story, there is still a deeper challenge you must face. You must willingly embrace the authority that comes with your new role, and learn to wield it with the confidence of Christ. This, too, is an exercise in faith, for you know full well the authority does not come from you and is not yours; it resides within the role to which God has called you. And yet, it is yours to wield. Indeed, God has chosen you to wield it. We are, in effect, stewards of God's power.

To do this effectively, you must relinquish your pet doubts about yourself, and radically believe—as God does—that you are the right person, at the right time, and in the right place to accomplish the role to which God has called you. You are not a poser. Your calling was not some Divine mistake. You are Joshua. You are Moses. You are Abraham and Esther and Samuel and Ruth and every other champion of God's glory and purpose throughout time. Not one of them accomplished their role in God's Story through their own authority or strength. Rather, through faith, they embraced and wielded the authority of God. And so must you.

The call of God is on your life. You have a key role in the grand Story of redemption he is telling in the world. Your role is unique. It is not a role for someone else. It is yours. But to truly live it out, you must stop doubting, and embrace it as your own.

MAKE IT REAL!

In your journal, write as much as you understand about the role God is calling you to fulfill in the world. After that, write five or six ways you could begin to step out more boldly in that role more boldly than you have so far. Then choose one and do it.

THE WAR FOR YOUR HEART
Week 3—Friday

Above all else, guard your heart, for it is the wellspring of life.
(Proverbs 4:23)

THERE is a battle being waged on your life. Something deep within you knows this, even though at times you struggle to see it clearly. But you know there is a battle because you feel its effects on many fronts—in your thoughts, your feelings, your relationships, your work, your health, your circumstances, even in your free time. You know when your life is under assault, even if you cannot see the attacker.

The truth is this: You have an enemy, and he has a goal. He is out to kill your heart.

By most standards, your enemy in this war is stronger than you are, and smarter. His tactics are proven, tested over several millennia of other battles he has fought and won. He never sleeps; he never stops the assault. He has devised a plan against you, and he is working right at this moment to carry it out.

And yet, he is afraid. He fears your heart—the very part of you he most wants to destroy. He knows that within your heart there lies a sleeping warrior waiting to be unleashed. And if the warrior is awakened, your enemy knows he cannot win. He cannot stand against a heart fully alive in the faith of Christ and the knowledge of his love. And so his only hope is to keep you ignorant, and sleeping.

MAKE IT REAL!

In your journal, describe where you see battle happening in your life right now. Why do you suppose the enemy is attacking those areas and not others? What is he really after here?

WEEKEND REFLECTION

TAKE a few moments this weekend to review the devotions you've read over this past week, as well as the "Make It Real!" steps you've done. As you reflect on the week, get curious about how God is moving in and through your life. Use these questions as a guide:

- ❖ What insights have you gained over the past week?
- ❖ What changes or shifts are you noticing in your relationship with God? with others? with yourself?
- ❖ What "Make It Real!" steps were the most meaningful for you? What made them meaningful?
- ❖ How will you live differently next week as a result of what you've learned?
- ❖ What support do you need to help you make that change?
- ❖ Based on your experiences over the past week, what do you most need from God right now?
- ❖ What do you suppose God might be wanting most from you right now?

CHALLENGE: If you missed one of the "Make It Real!" steps for this week, set aside time this weekend to complete it, and record your reactions, insights, and results in your journal.

*Guard the good deposit that was entrusted to you—guard it with
the help of the Holy Spirit who lives in us.*
(2 Timothy 1:14)

WHAT do you imagine would happen in the world if every
Christian were absolutely convinced to the core of their being
that Jesus truly loved them with his whole heart, and that his love
for them was unshakeable? If that were ever to actually happen—
and let us pray fervently that it does!—then we would
immediately be confronted with two powerful realizations. First,
we would realize that we are each stunningly beautiful, uniquely
endowed with splendor and grace—not because of anything we
have done, but because our Lord God Creator, who loves us, has
proclaimed us lovely. (His creative power, you'll recall, is
released through what he speaks.) Second, we would realize that
we are each created to do great things in the world—for we are
each entrusted to bear his glory, and that, by its very nature, is a
call to greatness.

Now, were this to happen, what do you suppose would
happen to Satan's reign of power on the earth? Simply stated, he
would be stopped. He would be trampled under the feet of the
Glorious Free. He would be forced to flee, and would lose his
stranglehold on the hearts of men and women everywhere our
feet trod.

It's time you understood why Satan strives so desperately to
keep your heart from living free. Because if you ever wake up to
the realization that you are loved, lovely, and called to a beautiful
greatness in the world, then he is finished. It is your heart—
awakened to its splendor and in love with Christ—that has the
power to stop him. His reign can only continue so long as you do
not see or live in the truth of who you truly are in the eyes of
God.

The essence of true spiritual warfare is this: to trust
unflinchingly in the love of God, to accept his proclamation of
who you truly are in your heart, and to build your life from *that*

place. For it is in your true heart that God has planted his glory and his purpose for your life, and only by living from there will you find the power to render the enemy impotent to stop you.

MAKE IT REAL!

How free and alive would you say your heart is these days? On a scale of 1 to 10, 10 being "totally alive and free," rate the level of aliveness and freedom your heart typically experiences in an average week. What's happening in your circumstances or environment to hold your heart at that level? Now, look deeper. What might be happening in the *spiritual realm* to hold your heart at that level? As a warrior in the Kingdom, what might God be calling you to do to in response to what you see happening in the Spirit?

For though we live in the world, we do not wage war as the world does. The weapons we fight with are not the weapons of the world. On the contrary, they have divine power to demolish strongholds. We demolish arguments and every pretension that sets itself up against the knowledge of God, and we take captive every thought to make it obedient to Christ.
(2 Corinthians 10:3-5)

THE enemy employs a wide assortment of strategies in his schemes to defeat you. He may, for example, come against your finances. He may attack your health. He may stir up friction in your family or between you and your closest friends. But whatever the external focus of the attack, the ultimate target is always the same. The enemy is trying to *wound your heart*. He knows your heart holds the key to his defeat, and so he spends all of his energy trying to keep it distracted, weary, and confused.

Through his relentless, varied, and often subtle attacks on your life, your enemy will try to disconnect you from your heart so that you lose touch with who you really are. He will try to numb your heart so that you no longer feel your own passion or much of anything else. He will try to convince you that your heart is flawed beyond repair, that it is unredeemed and unredeemable so that you will hide yourself from love. He will try to convince you that your heart is weak and cannot be trusted so you will learn to hate it. He will try to convince you that your heart is undesirable and plain so you will live in desperation for the approval of those you deem more worthy than yourself. He will try to convince you that God doesn't really love you (though he loves everyone else), or that he is deeply disappointed in how your heart turned out so you will strive to win his approval through your performance. He will try to convince you that your heart has no purpose in the world, no meaning in this life, and no reason to keep resisting his assault.

Do any of these scenarios feel familiar? Then know that war in the heavens has been waged over you, and is being waged still.

Your heart is the prize at stake. And the only way to win the battle is to keep your vigilance focused there.

What lies have you historically believed about your own heart? Make a quick list of them in your journal. As you read through them, are there any you are still believing today—even a little? Place an asterisk next to any that feel suspiciously current. Then get together with a trusted Christian ally and share your list. Don't rush through it—really take your time in explaining how these lies have snared your heart. Then ask your friend to pray with you for God to fill your heart with a greater revelation of his love for you and his truth about who you are in him.

Put on the full armor of God so that you can take your stand against the devil's schemes. For our struggle is not against flesh and blood, but against the rulers, against the authorities, against the powers of this dark world and against the spiritual forces of evil in the heavenly realms. Therefore put on the full armor of God, so that when the day of evil comes, you may be able to stand your ground, and after you have done everything, to stand.
(Ephesians 6:11-13)

SPIRITUAL warfare is ultimately about uprooting lies, and calling forth God's truth to rule and reign in the world. God has provided his own armor to equip you for that fight, but you aren't likely to embrace the discipline of donning it every day until you realize that the spiritual battle is not just happening "over there" on some distance front. You *are* the front. And every day you do not equip yourself for the fight, your heart suffers harm.

The battle for your heart is real. It is happening. It is upon you. And no amount of wishing it otherwise will change that fact. If you do not open your eyes and consciously engage the fight, you will automatically forfeit the victory in life that could be yours…that by all rights in Christ *should* be yours.

You are a warrior for the Kingdom of God, and no other saint can fight the battle to which you have been called. It is your path, your calling, your purpose, your "good fight of faith" (1 Timothy 6:12). No one else can fight it for you, nor spare you from the struggle it entails. In order to win, you must first say yes to the battle.

But once you open your heart to the course ahead, and take up the armor, the sword and shield, and stand your ground against the enemy's assaults upon your life, you will find a strength of faith unleashed within your heart, springing up from the fountain of God's immeasurable love for you. And you will understand, perhaps in a way you never have before, that you truly are worth fighting for.

What is the current battle that God is calling you to fight? Name it. Then take some time to create a strategic plan for the battle. Include a list of biblically-sound tactics for both attack and defense. For ideas on what some of these might be, consult the "Spiritual Warfare Verses" list. When your plan is complete, commit to follow it every day for the next 30 days. At the end of that time, schedule some time alone with God to examine the outcome of your actions. What worked? What didn't? What's changed?

SPIRITUAL WARFARE VERSES
 2 Corinthians 6:1-7
 Ephesians 4:25-27
 Ephesians 5:7-17
 Ephesians 6:10-18
 1 Timothy 6:11-12
 2 Timothy 2:3-4
 James 4:7-8
 1 Peter 5:8-9
 1 John 5:4-5

THE JESUS WE NEED TO KNOW
Week 4—Thursday

*Your attitude should be the same as that of Christ Jesus: Who,
being in very nature God, did not consider equality with God
something to be grasped, but made himself nothing, taking the
very nature of a servant, being made in human likeness. And
being found in appearance as a man, he humbled himself and
became obedient to death—even death on a cross!*
(Philippians 2:5-8)

IT is an amazing thing that God became human. I'm not referring
to the miracle of the act itself—God limiting his power and
control of the universe, God taking on the form and attributes of
something he created—as mind-boggling as all that is. I'm
talking about the love. Imagine a love so large, so unquenchable
and undeniable, that it could compel a perfect, self-sufficient, all-
powerful Being like God to become one of us—for no other
reason than to woo us to him in a way we could understand. From
the beginning of time until this very moment, there has never
been a more passionate or more abandoned act of pure desire
than the appearance of Jesus on earth.

Christ came so that we might know God. Not know of him,
not know about him. But truly *know him.* Jesus came to show you
who God is, what God is like, and to provide a way for you to
come to him unafraid—in the singular hope that you might fall in
love with him, just as he has already most certainly fallen in love
with you.

MAKE IT REAL!

In your journal, write a prayer to Jesus describing who he is to
you. You might start each sentence with something like, "Jesus,
you are my…" or "Jesus, you are to me a…" Don't fall into
cliché, or write what you think you "ought" to say. Instead, really
answer the question: "Who is Jesus *to you personally?*"

THE PERFECT REPRESENTATION
Week 4—Friday

*The Son is the radiance of God's glory and the exact
representation of his being, sustaining all things by his powerful
word. After he had provided purification for sins, he sat down at
the right hand of the Majesty in heaven.*
(Hebrews 1:3)

CHRISTIANS often make a fuss about making Jesus too
familiar, too much like us. They say that focusing too closely on
his humanity will dilute our sense of his holiness, and tempt us to
treat God as more of a chummy pal than as the Lord of our lives.
And yet, it was not our idea to humanize God—it was God's idea
to humanize himself. Jesus—the God Man—is the perfect
revelation of who God is. The amazing truth is that Christ's
humanity reveals to us as much about God's nature as his divinity
does. For while his divinity let us know that Jesus is God, his
humanity let us know that God is a Person—a Person who longs
to be known.

To know that Jesus is righteous, that he is holy, that he is
loving and wise is merely the first step toward truly knowing him
in the way he wants to be known. The prophets and patriarchs of
the Old Testament knew all about these attributes of God, and
many others. But they longed for more. After Moses had received
God's commandments on Mount Sinai, he cried out, "Now show
me your glory" (Exodus 33:18). But God showed Moses only his
back. It is only in Jesus that Moses' prayer is fully answered. For
only in Jesus do we finally see God's face. "The Son is the
radiance of God's glory and the exact representation of his
being."

Through Jesus, we come to know God as a Person. We see
the way he moves through the world. We observe what he
responds to and what he ignores. We watch him demonstrate
what really matters to him through his actions and his words, as
well as through his silence and what he chooses not to do.
Through Jesus, we experience God firsthand, living among us.

Without such a personal experience of God, there can be no true intimacy or friendship.

And that, after all, is what God is after. For Jesus didn't come to earth looking for servants. He came looking for friends.

MAKE IT REAL!

Do you consider yourself to be God's friend? If you could have any sort of friendship with God you wanted, what would it look like? Write a description of your ideal friendship with God, then ask God to show you what kind of friendship *he wants with you.*

WEEKEND REFLECTION

TAKE a few moments this weekend to review the devotions you've read over this past week, as well as the "Make It Real!" steps you've done. As you reflect on the week, get curious about how God is moving in and through your life. Use these questions as a guide:

❖ What insights have you gained over the past week?
❖ What changes or shifts are you noticing in your relationship with God? with others? with yourself?
❖ What "Make It Real!" steps were the most meaningful for you? What made them meaningful?
❖ How will you live differently next week as a result of what you've learned?
❖ What support do you need to help you make that change?
❖ Based on your experiences over the past week, what do you most need from God right now?
❖ What do you suppose God might be wanting most from you right now?

CHALLENGE: If you missed one of the "Make It Real!" steps for this week, set aside time this weekend to complete it, and record your reactions, insights, and results in your journal.

Jesus answered: "Don't you know me, Philip,
even after I have been among you such a long time?"
(John 14:9)

JESUS asks many of us the same question he asked of Philip in the final days of his life: "Don't you know me…even after I have been among you such a long time?" Our churches have taught us how to go to Jesus to ask for the things we need or desire for ourselves or those we love. But most of them never taught us the most important task of all—how to go to Jesus with no other goal than simply to know him.

What does it look like to get to know Jesus in this way—simply as one person getting to know Another? The answer begins as it does with any relationship, with simple curiosity. As you read the Gospel accounts of Jesus' life, what intrigues you about the man Jesus Christ? What does he do that surprises you? What does he say—or not say—that strikes you as odd or even silly? Wherever that curiosity surfaces, begin there.

For example, have you ever wondered how often Jesus laughed? Was he always somber—as the popular notion of him would have us believe—or was he upbeat, even silly at times? If so, what made him chuckle? We don't often think of Jesus as having a sense of humor—which is ridiculous really, since he invented humor.

More examples: Have you ever been curious about Jesus' favorite time of day, or his favorite season? Was he close to his parents? to his siblings? As he and the disciples traveled together, what did they talk about around the campfire at night? When Jesus went off alone to pray, what did he pray about?

Once you have a list of your own curious questions, don't simply ponder them in silence. Pray them. If you do, you will be amazed at the joy Jesus takes in revealing his answers to you.

As you read through the Gospels to create your list of "curious questions," keep your focus on "getting to know Jesus." Look at the stories through Jesus' perspective, rather than your own. For example, when you read about Jesus feeding the 5,000, instead of asking, "What is this story saying about how I should live?" ask questions that focus on Jesus. "What prompted Jesus to feed the 5,000? Why did he go about it the way he did? What made him so angry after it was over? What does this story tell me about Jesus as a Person? What questions does it leave unanswered?"

*In bringing many sons to glory, it was fitting that God, for whom
and through whom everything exists, should make the author of
their salvation perfect through suffering. Both the one who makes
men holy and those who are made holy are of the same family. So
Jesus is not ashamed to call them brothers.*
(Hebrews 2:10-11)

IMAGINE for a moment that Jesus is your older brother. I
mean your real, flesh-and-blood brother who grew up in your
home, and has been with you since your earliest memory of
family. Now suppose that you knew—that you *really knew*—that
this brother of yours named Jesus loves you more than his own
life. He is constantly looking out for your best interests, gladly
sacrifices for you, and is determined to see you become all you
can be—all because he loves you. If that were true, what do you
imagine your relationship with Jesus would be like?

For every Christ follower, that is the true nature of your
relationship with Jesus, even if you don't realize it, or perhaps
don't believe it. But your lack of awareness or faith does not keep
Jesus from loving you. He is not ashamed of his love for you, and
proclaims it through his every thought and act, whether you are
willing to see it or not.

"I want to see it," you may say, "but I just don't. God's love
just doesn't seem that real to me." Then get curious about it. Ask
Jesus to tell you about his love for you. But when you do, be
specific. For example, what really draws Jesus to *you* in
particular? What does he find especially attractive about you?
What is it in you that draws him? What does he love about your
personality? about your humor? about the way you think? When
he intercedes for you in heaven, what specifically does he ask?

Jesus came as the perfect revelation of who God is. But he
also came as a man. And it's through his humanity that we find
the connection we need to make God's love real in our lives.
Jesus' arrival was and is an invitation to an intimate communion
between our hearts and God's. By accepting the invitation to get

to know the man Jesus—as a Person who loves you and longs to be loved and known in return—you will find over time, just as Philip did, that you know God.

MAKE IT REAL!

Take a day-long retreat alone with Jesus, and prayerfully journal your responses to each of the questions listed on the previous page. What do your responses reveal about your perceptions of Jesus? about your perceptions of yourself?

LOSING OUR WAY ON THE ROAD TO LIFE
Week 5—Wednesday

But small is the gate and narrow
the road that leads to life,
and only a few find it.
(Matthew 7:14)

DON'T think that just because you have found the road that
leads to life that that's all there is to it. Finding the road—
entering into a relationship with Jesus—is only the start, the
beginning place of the journey to attain a life of true abundance
in Christ. Which is why, of course, Jesus calls it a "road," and not
a destination. The road itself is not life—which is to say it is not
the end goal. Rather, it is the path of faith and discovery that
leads us to life. True redemption, in Jesus' terms, is always a
heroic journey—from what you once were to what God created
you to be when he lovingly dreamed of you before the making of
the world. That sort of transformation is a severe and serious
thing. It takes heart—and courage—to embrace a quest like that.

It's no wonder, then, that so many Christians have lost their
way on the road to life. They've lost heart, and along with it, any
sense of direction. They're on the road, but they're heading
nowhere in particular. Like the Israelites in the desert of Sinai,
they wander aimlessly from one side to the other, frustrated and
wondering why this "new life in Christ" doesn't seem to be all it
was cracked up to be. For them, the Christian life has become
marked by a stagnant struggle between what is and what ought to
be. I ought to be content and peaceful, but I'm not. I ought to be
delivered from the power of sin, but I am not. I ought to be
fulfilled and full of joy, but I am not. They're stuck on the road,
wrongly thinking that it's the destination. The road is narrow, and
only a few find it. But the sad truth is that even fewer ever find
the abundant life to which it leads.

If you have found the road that leads to life—wonderful!
Now God is asking you a different question: Now that you're on
the road, what do you desire? Are you ready to courageously
embrace the journey—to press forward toward the fulfillment of

all the promises God has spoken over you? Are you ready to go after the life God meant for you to live? If so, then it's time to stop staring at your shoes on the road and fix your gaze on the "life to the full" that's waiting for you down the way.

MAKE IT REAL!

Where are you on the road to life? Have you arrived at your desired destination? Are you halfway there? Have you stalled just beyond the gate? Draw a horizontal line on a sheet of paper. At one end, write "The gate—meeting Jesus" and at the other end write "Totally fulfilling abundant life in Christ." Then place an X at the position along the line that you think best represents where you are on the road right now. Imagine what it would take for your life to move just one step closer to a totally fulfilling abundant life in Christ. Write it out as a goal, and ask God to grant you the courage and determination to begin taking that one step forward this week.

If someone claims, "I belong to God,"
but doesn't obey God's commandments,
that person is a liar and does not live in the truth.
(1 John 2:4, NLT)

LET'S say you are going to Hollywood this weekend. Just a quick, fun getaway, nothing too elaborate. Maybe you're going because you got tickets to be a part of the studio audience for the live season finale of your favorite TV show—perhaps a reality show like *American Idol* or *Survivor* or one of the other dozen or so shows like it. Anyway, the tickets are free, and the hotel wasn't that expensive, so why not?

But while you're there, a TV producer walks up to you and makes you an incredible offer. He'll pay you $250,000 if you'll allow him to videotape your life for 30 days. He'll do the filming over the next six months, and you won't have to do anything special—just live your life as you normally would. The only catch is that the videotaping will be done in secret. You won't know when you're being filmed until the show airs at the start of next season.

Would you do it? And if you did, what do you think would be the result? What would the videotape reveal about your life and the way you live it? What message or messages would your life-on-tape bring to the world?

What would you learn about yourself? And most important of all—what would you discover about your heart?

MAKE IT REAL!

Over the coming week, pay attention to the way you are living your life. At the end of each day, journal your honest responses to these questions:

- ❖ What did I spend the bulk of my energy on today?
- ❖ What issues dominated my thoughts?
- ❖ What beliefs dominated my life today?

At the end of the week, review your answers, then prayerfully consider how you'd answer this question: What is the overall message my life is broadcasting to the world?

So we are lying if we say we have fellowship with God but go on living in spiritual darkness. We are not living in the truth.
(1 John 1:6, NLT)

THE truth of the matter is this: We live what we believe. We all live our beliefs—each one of us, every day, without exception. That is why Jesus made it clear that the way to know a person's heart was to look at the fruit of his or her life. "By their fruit you will recognize them. Do people pick grapes from thornbushes, or figs from thistles? Likewise every good tree bears good fruit, but a bad tree bears bad fruit" (Matthew 7:16-17). The same is true of you. Your "fruit" reveals your heart as well. So what would a videotape of your life reveal about what you really believe?

For example, it does no good to say, "I believe God is trustworthy" if your life is filled with worry. You do not really believe God is trustworthy—that is, that you can *actually trust him*—or else your heart would not be full of worry. You may wish you trusted God, you may intellectually believe it is the right thing to do, but that is not the same thing as actually doing it. The way you live reveals your beliefs more truly than any prayer of confession or statement of doctrine.

Do you believe that God loves you and accepts you in the Beloved? Then why do you struggle with self-acceptance? If the King and Ruler of the Universe has declared you Lovable and Acceptable, and even Beautiful and Beloved—why do you find yourself still questioning your own worth, or worry over whether others find you acceptable or "good enough"? You see, the problem is not in God's power to make you acceptable and beautiful; the problem is in you not really believing it, even though you say you do.

It is this self-deception that robs us of the power of God. We will never truly believe—and therefore, never experience the true power of God—until we are willing to be gut-wrenchingly honest with ourselves. Examine your life—see what it tells you about what you really believe. Then ask yourself the question that Jesus asked Peter in the storm. "Why do you doubt?"

An honest answer to that question will mark your next profound step toward freedom.

MAKE IT REAL!

At the top of a blank sheet of paper, write this opening: "I'm afraid that…" Then fill the page with everything that comes to mind. Don't stop until you can't think of anything else. What do your responses say about what you really believe about God, his love for you, or his purpose for your life?

TAKE a few moments this weekend to review the devotions you've read over this past week, as well as the "Make It Real!" steps you've done. As you reflect on the week, get curious about how God is moving in and through your life. Use these questions as a guide:

- ❖ What insights have you gained over the past week?
- ❖ What changes or shifts are you noticing in your relationship with God? with others? with yourself?
- ❖ What "Make It Real!" steps were the most meaningful for you? What made them meaningful?
- ❖ How will you live differently next week as a result of what you've learned?
- ❖ What support do you need to help you make that change?
- ❖ Based on your experiences over the past week, what do you most need from God right now?
- ❖ What do you suppose God might be wanting most from you right now?

CHALLENGE: If you missed one of the "Make It Real!" steps for this week, set aside time this weekend to complete it, and record your reactions, insights, and results in your journal.

AN HONEST APPRAISAL OF OUR FAITH
Week 6—Monday

Now faith is being sure of what we hope for
and certain of what we do not see.
(Hebrews 11:1)

WANTING to believe the truth is good—but that is only the first step toward faith. Many Christians live powerless lives because they mistake the wanting to believe for belief itself. Wanting says, "I hope God will provide for me," or "I hope God will show me he loves me." But faith is "the assurance of things hoped for." Faith isn't in the wishing, but in the determined courageous choice to know a thing is true. Faith is surrendering to the truth and love you cannot see; it is jumping off the cliff into the arms of the Invisible But Real. Faith doesn't merely hope. Faith knows.

The power of the redeemed life in Christ comes only to those who have let go of the right to deceive themselves. They do not sever the power of God by claiming to believe truths they do not yet embrace. They are honest, even when their honesty is disillusioning. If you are struggling with fear that God won't come through for you, that he does not see you, that he does not really care for your heart, then stop pretending you are firm in your beliefs and get honest with yourself and with God. If you deceive yourself into thinking you already believe as you should, then what will you do with the fear that still grips you? There is nothing left for it but to beg God to take it away, or to bring you whatever gift you think will cancel it out. But God will not likely do as you ask—his love for you constrains him. For he knows the root of your fear is not in the absence of whatever you are longing for; the fear lies in your unbelief. Even if he brought you the thing you wanted, the fear would not go away because the unbelief would remain.

Stop focusing on the external things. The thing you lack is not in the world, but in your heart. Stop merely wanting to believe, and move your heart closer to true freedom. Make the choice to actually believe. Choose him.

MAKE IT REAL!

Go to three friends who know you well, and ask them to share their honest, raw, unfiltered response to this question: Based on what you know of my life, what would you say are the most prominent beliefs my life projects to the world?

THE INTIMATE DANCE OF TRUST
Week 6—Tuesday

Whoever claims to live in him must walk as Jesus did.
(1 John 2:6)

SOCRATES once wrote that "the unexamined life is not worth living." How much more true this is for the Christian who wants to walk in the power of God! For you can never move to a place of greater power in your walk with Jesus until you know exactly where you stand with him right now. And the only way to know that is to examine your life—and learn what it has to teach you about what you really believe.

Think for a moment about your common day. As you move through the hours, what do you notice about your heart? Is it present or more often subdued beneath the stresses of deadlines and "to dos"? What about your thoughts—where do they go, what do they dwell on as the day progresses? Where does your energy go? What are you focused on most of the time? What stresses you about your day? What angers you? What makes you laugh? What do the efforts of your day bring to the world? What is your life producing?

All of these questions lead to one that under girds them all: *What truth am I actually living?*

We claim to live in Christ, but, in fact, very few of us ever do—or even really think about how such a life might look in our frenetic work-a-day world. But it is a question we must consciously explore if we are ever to truly live in Christ in a way that brings life to our hearts and to the broken places of the world. The Apostle John described such a life in simple elegance—"Whoever claims to live in him must walk as Jesus did." But his description implies far more than mimicry. He is talking about a communion, a unity of hearts—Christ's and yours. It is an intimate dance, and Jesus is the lead.

What does that life look like for you? I don't know. But you do—deep in your heart, you do. You always have. It's the life you've always longed for, yet hesitated to step into for fear it wouldn't prove real. But what if it was? What if it is yours for the choosing? What then?

MAKE IT REAL!

What would an "intimate life with Christ" look like for you if you could live it every day? Take some time to journal about this new vision for your life. What would you do when you wake up in the morning? What would you do next? And after that? What kinds of words would people use to describe your life? What impact would your life have on the people around you? Create a word picture of what that life would be like, and begin to ask God to show you how to move toward making it real in practical ways.

DANCING WITH ALL YOUR MIGHT
Week 6—Wednesday

David...danced before the Lord with all his might.
(2 Samuel 6:14)

PEOPLE often marvel that David felt free to dance with such abandon before the Lord in the sight of all his people, even though he was a king. But the truth is that he was made a king by God precisely *because* his heart was willing to dance in this way—with raw, unfettered, passionate devotion to God. The Lord made this clear from the moment of David's anointing. "Man looks at the outward appearance," God told Samuel, "but the Lord looks at the heart" (1 Samuel 16:7). David's heart was willing to dance before God with all of his might. And so the anointing came to him.

Life with Jesus is a dance—a daily interplay of his Spirit with ours, the subtle lead and follow of his gentle pressing and our surrender to the movements of his hand. Or so it is meant to be. But often we resist his lead, or lose sight of him altogether in the distractions of lesser matters.

Consider your life—the way you are living right now before God. What sort of dance are you dancing with him? If you had to name it, what kind of dance would it be? A dance of fear, timidity, or hesitation? A dance of surrender, might, wild abandon? Or something in between?

Now, consider this: What would it look like for you to dance before the Lord with all of your might? I am not speaking only of literal dancing—but rather the dance of your daily life with him. If you stepped into the dance of life with God as David did, what kind of dance would that be? What kind of music would accompany you and your Lord as you moved across the floor? What sort of impact would your dance with Jesus have on the world?

MAKE IT REAL!

Take some time with your journal and dream a little. If your daily life with God *were* a dance, what sort of dance would you want it to be? What effect would the dance have on you? On the people watching you? What message would your dance with God bring to the world?

FROM FEAR TO UNDERSTANDING
Week 6—Thursday

Love the Lord your God
with all your heart
and with all your soul
and with all your mind
and with all your strength.
(Mark 12:30)

WHAT is it to love God in this way—with all of your heart, all of your soul, all of your mind, and all of your strength? We all agree it should be done—that we should do it—but when it comes down to the level of daily life, our vision for what it actually looks like quite often grows fuzzy and indistinct. We often secretly think it is impractical. We have obligations to attend to. We have bills, chores, stresses, and deadlines all of which demand a portion of our strength and focus. It would be nice to give God everything all the time, but it just can't be done. Perhaps when we get to heaven, we will know that sort of life, but for now we must content ourselves with glimpses and dreams, and hope for a time when we have more time.

But that is only a justification. For the deeper reality is that we are afraid. Afraid to relinquish control on such a grand scale. Afraid that we will not follow well. Afraid that God will not lead well. Afraid that, in the end, our attempt to dance with him with all our might will only make us look foolish on the stage of the world, and make a train wreck of our lives.

There is no shame in being afraid. There has never been a mighty man or woman of God who has not faced down fear in the course of following God. The danger comes in refusing to recognize the fear is there, to make believe there is some other reason why you will not step into the wild, abandoned dance that God is inviting you to share with him.

The first step to freedom is to recognize your bonds.

MAKE IT REAL!

What fears do you have around loving God with all your heart? If you did love God in that way, what's the worst that could happen? What's the best? Go to a trusted Christian ally and tell him or her about your fears. Ask him or her to pray with you, asking God to give you the courage you need to really step into the dance.

FROM OBLIGATION TO FREE CHOICE
Week 6—Friday

I belong to my lover, and his desire is for me.
(Song of Songs 7:10)

WHEN at first we hear the command to "love the Lord your God with all your heart and with all your soul and with all your mind and with all your strength" (Mark 12:30), our own minds typically move to places of obligation and duty. "Jesus died for me, so I owe it to him to love him and obey his commands. It's the least I can do after all he's done for me." And off we go looking for lists of things we can do to show him we are towing the line, to demonstrate that we are stand-up men and women of God, to establish that we are good Christian people. The problem with this line of reasoning is that no one has ever fallen in love out of obligation. And so long as we think that God's command to love him stems from a sort of "you owe Me this" mentality on his part, we will never really love him as he desires, and we will never truly understand his heart.

Love is always a free choice. It must always be a free choice—without fear of punishment or reprisal—or else it cannot truly be love. Who wants to be loved out of obligation? I don't, and I seriously doubt you do either. Is it any surprise then, that God wants our love for him to be something more as well?

So what is it to love God in the way he desires? As with any love, it begins by understanding the core desires of his heart. "I belong to my lover, and his desire is for me." The entire story of the Bible—from the first scenes with Adam and Eve, to the final scene of the New Jerusalem coming down from heaven—is the story of a Lover wooing his Beloved, simply because he wants to love her. He wants to know her, and to make himself known. He wants to share life together. The story of the Bible is, in essence, God's invitation to dance.

When at last we understand this, we will find that whatever fear we have had in surrendering our lives to him disappears. For once you see his heart, you begin to understand at last that the Majestic Creator of the Universe does not love you because of what you do or don't do for him; he loves you because he sees your heart, and thinks it beautiful.

MAKE IT REAL!

In your journal, make a list of all the things you "do for God" in a typical week. This may include things like "go to church," "share my faith with others," "choose not to strangle my annoying co-worker," and so on. Next, create a new list—this time, think only of *things you would love to do* to show your love for God. It may be something as simple as writing a song, or as elaborate as working with orphans in a third-world country. The only rule is that it must be something you would truly enjoy doing. When you're finished, compare your lists. What do you notice? What's one "love to do" thing you can begin pursuing this week?

WEEKEND REFLECTION

TAKE a few moments this weekend to review the devotions you've read over this past week, as well as the "Make It Real!" steps you've done. As you reflect on the week, get curious about how God is moving in and through your life. Use these questions as a guide:

- ❖ What insights have you gained over the past week?
- ❖ What changes or shifts are you noticing in your relationship with God? with others? with yourself?
- ❖ What "Make It Real!" steps were the most meaningful for you? What made them meaningful?
- ❖ How will you live differently next week as a result of what you've learned?
- ❖ What support do you need to help you make that change?
- ❖ Based on your experiences over the past week, what do you most need from God right now?
- ❖ What do you suppose God might be wanting most from you right now?

CHALLENGE: If you missed one of the "Make It Real!" steps for this week, set aside time this weekend to complete it, and record your reactions, insights, and results in your journal.

Trust in the Lord with all your heart and lean not on your own
understanding; in all your ways acknowledge him, and he will
make your paths straight.
(Proverbs 3:5-6)

THE word for "acknowledge" in this verse is *yada.* In the most
basic sense, it means to "know"—as in, "in all your ways, know
him, and he will make your paths straight." But that is only the
beginning of the riches this single word holds. The rest of the
definition goes something like this: "to know (properly to
ascertain by *seeing*), to be aware of, to recognize, to watch for, to
discover, to befriend, to make yourself known to, to learn from."
And so we see that the word *yada* does not merely refer to a
cursory nod to God's presence in our lives, but is a description of
an intimate awareness and communion between our hearts and
God's.

Take it a step further, and expand other key words in the
passage, and what you get is a beautiful depiction of our daily
relationship with God—as *he* desires it to be: *Boldly trust and*
place your confidence in the Lord with all your heart and do not
rely or rest in your own knowledge, wisdom, or understanding. In
any and every road you take—both great and small—look for
God and see him, recognize him, watch him, be aware of him,
discover him, befriend him, make yourself known to him, reveal
yourself to him, and learn from him—and he will make your
paths straight, pleasant, and prosperous.

Do this, and you will no longer have to wonder what it would
look like for you to dance with all your might before God as
David did. For your own dance with Jesus will have already
begun.

MAKE IT REAL!

What would it look like for you start dancing with Jesus this week in your daily life? What's the first thing you would need to do? the second? And then what? Make a list of steps to move you from where you are in your connection with God to where you really want to be. Then, for the rest of this month, commit yourself to taking one step each week toward the kind of relationship with Jesus that he desires to have with you.

God said to Moses, "I am who I am. This is what you are to say
to the Israelites: 'I AM has sent me to you.'"
(Exodus 3:14)

IMAGINE the scene: A wizened but wary Moses, standing
barefoot and afraid before a bush ablaze with fire but not
consumed. And from this fiery miracle, a Voice resounds—
strong and resolute, unlike any the man has ever heard. He's
more than 80 years old now, and this is the first time God has
spoken to him. This is the moment God has chosen to reveal
himself—through miraculous fire, through a Voice, and a Name.
  "I AM..."
  Of all the names for himself that God could reveal in this
moment—Almighty, Compassionate, All-Knowing, King of
Kings—he chooses this one, "I AM," as the most critical name
for God that Moses needs to hear. But why this name? What is
God wanting Moses to understand about his character and his
ways? Certainly, that he is the Self-Existent One, dependent on
no one and nothing for his eternal life and identity. But also, and
just as critical, that he is God of the Present Moment; that "Right
Now" is where he lives.
  Do you ever wonder where God is in your life? The answer is
always the same: He is right here next to you, revealing himself
to you in this present moment. If you cannot find him, it is not
because he has gone anywhere. When God seems distant, the real
question, the one you should be asking, is this: "Where am I?"

MAKE IT REAL!

Take a moment to get in touch with where your heart is right now. What is occupying your mind right now? What are you feeling? How do you feel in your body right now? Create a mental "snapshot" of where you are, right at this moment. Focus on setting aside anything that isn't tied to this moment, right now, and just let yourself be *here*. Then invite God to join you in this present moment. As you do this, what do you notice?

Be still, and know that I am God...
(Psalm 46:10)

WE are not commanded to be still so that we can focus our energy on properly imagining that God is somewhere nearby, watching over us from a distance in his paternal way. Rather, stillness is a prerequisite for recognizing what is already here— that is, that God is *actually, truthfully, with you right now*. He is the God of the past, the present, and the future. But he always manifests himself in this present moment—and *never* any other time or place.

The word *know* in Psalm 46:10 means to "ascertain by seeing." Generally, when we do not see God, it is because we are looking somewhere other than the present. We are worried about the future, so our focus is there. We are regretting the past, so our focus is there. Meanwhile, God is asking you to be still, to come back to this moment, right now, and see that he is right here with you.

To be still means to lay down your busy worries about the future or nagging regrets about the past, and simply make yourself aware of your heart and life in this present moment. Look around. Notice what is happening in the space around you at this moment. Notice what you are feeling, what you are thinking—right now. And in your noticing, you will soon recognize that God is here as well—as his Spirit always is, present and ready to love you in this moment.

MAKE IT REAL!

Take some time today—even if it's just 15 minutes—to focus on becoming present and still. Go to a quiet, reflective place where you won't be disturbed. Turn off the television and the mp3 player or radio. Spend a few minutes with your eyes closed, and focus on nothing but your breath. Just "be." When your mind has quieted, invite God to join you in the present moment; then open your eyes and look around. What do you notice that you weren't aware of before? What is the gift God has for you in this moment?

*Therefore, since we have been justified through faith, we have
peace with God through our Lord Jesus Christ, through whom we
have gained access by faith into this grace in which we now
stand. And we rejoice in the hope of the glory of God.*
(Romans 5:1-2)

GRACE—that is, the power to live the Christian life—is always
given as a capacity to live fully in this present moment. We do
not get grace for tomorrow while it is still today, anymore than
the Israelites could gather more manna than each day required.
The walk of faith and intimacy with God is a walk in the present.
It is no wonder, then, that Jesus admonished us keep our focus on
the here and now. "Do not worry about tomorrow, for tomorrow
will worry about itself. *Each day has enough trouble of its own"*
(Matthew 6:34).

The grace that the Holy Spirit gives us in each moment is *for
that moment* alone. To live by grace, then, requires that we learn
how to live "present" lives, and not allow our hearts to be
consumed with worry over things that have happened in the past
or things that might happen tomorrow, neither of which are
within our control. Your life is not in the past or in the future.
Your life is right now. Why not be here while it happens? For
"right now" is where God is waiting to live it with you. And
"right now" is the only place you will find his grace, his peace,
and his victory.

This is the way God has designed our life with him, so that
the goal of life will not become to "just get through the struggle"
or "achieve the goal"—but rather, to know God intimately and
walk with him from moment to moment.

MAKE IT REAL!

In your journal, list all of the things that are troubling you these days—from issues at work, to issues with friends or family, to your finances, or your love life. When you're finished, go back through the list and circle every item that revolves around something that has happened in the past or might happen in the future. Prayerfully release each of those future/past items into God's hands. Consciously let them go. Then bring the "present" items to God and ask for his grace to come into the moment and give you strength. As you do this, what do you notice about your heart? How would your life change if you did this every day?

THE "I AM" OF GOD'S PRESENCE
Week 7—Friday

...surely I am with you always, to the very end of the age.
(Matthew 28:20)

THERE is great spiritual power in being present, because the present is where Jesus is. But there is also much more than power alone—for everything that Jesus is, is here in this moment, as well. His joy, his peace, his wisdom and insight, his acceptance and unfathomable love for you—all of these are spread before you like a banquet from one moment to the next. Once we begin to recognize the sufficiency of Christ's presence with us in this moment, we find that we don't want to be anywhere else—even when the present moment is also full of sorrow or trials. The abiding presence of Christ in our lives becomes not only our refuge, but also our sustenance and our joy. *Being with him right now is what matters.* Once our hearts come to realize that singular truth, the trials, no matter how deep or severe, no longer have the power to make us afraid.

"God is our refuge and strength, an ever-present help in trouble. Therefore we will not fear, though the earth give way and the mountains fall into the heart of the sea, though its waters roar and foam and the mountains quake with their surging" (Psalm 46:1-3).

That is not to say that we do not wish the trial to be over, or that we do not pray that it end. But the trial no longer has the power to rule us, for we have found a Strength and Love in this present moment that is more than a match for the struggle we face. Victory is simply being with him, right now, in the midst of it all. That is the heart of deliverance.

MAKE IT REAL!

For the next seven days, make it your ambition to be completely present wherever you are. To begin, create a word picture of what "being completely present" would look like for you. Does it mean giving all you have to whatever is in front of you each moment of the day? Or might it include taking time throughout the day to notice your surroundings, to look out the window and take it all in, or to listen to your own body? Where does prayer fit into your vision? Once you create your portrait of a "present life," go after it. Perhaps you might use a reminder to help you do this, such as wearing a rubber band around your wrist or placing a sign on your desk that says "Be here." As you go through the week, keep a journal of your experience. What's hard about being present? What is it teaching you? How has your experience of God changed in this process? When the week is over, share your discoveries with a trusted friend, and tell him or her how this experience will change the way you live from now on.

TAKE a few moments this weekend to review the devotions you've read over this past week, as well as the "Make It Real!" steps you've done. As you reflect on the week, get curious about how God is moving in and through your life. Use these questions as a guide:

- ❖ What insights have you gained over the past week?
- ❖ What changes or shifts are you noticing in your relationship with God? with others? with yourself?
- ❖ What "Make It Real!" steps were the most meaningful for you? What made them meaningful?
- ❖ How will you live differently next week as a result of what you've learned?
- ❖ What support do you need to help you make that change?
- ❖ Based on your experiences over the past week, what do you most need from God right now?
- ❖ What do you suppose God might be wanting most from you right now?

CHALLENGE: If you missed one of the "Make It Real!" steps for this week, set aside time this weekend to complete it, and record your reactions, insights, and results in your journal.

THE PRACTICE OF SOLITUDE
Week 8—Monday

Then, because so many people were coming and going that they did not even have a chance to eat, he said to them, "Come with me by yourselves to a quiet place and get some rest."
(Mark 6:31)

WHEN you hear the word *solitude,* what feeling does it evoke in you? Splendor, wonderment, intimacy, joy? Absolute delight? Excitement and expectation?

Yeah. Not likely.

For many, solitude is our secret nemesis. Though we may not speak of it often, it is never far from our thoughts. Each of us, in our own way, works hard every week to fight it off with the same zeal we apply to fighting off sickness or poverty. We fill our schedules with social engagements, keep ourselves busy to the point of exhaustion, and fill our minds with reality TV or news or music or books—often not even realizing the powerful influence our aversion to solitude is having on our choices. We may not actually want such frenetically busy lives. But at least it's better than the alternative. Isn't it?

We tend to associate seasons of solitude with loneliness, isolation and even hopelessness. So it is perhaps no wonder that when Jesus beckons us away to spend time alone, we often resist the call. But when at last we answer, we are surprised to find that the solitude Jesus wants for us is not a futile exercise in loneliness, but rather a life-giving practice that enriches our hearts with the powerful gifts of clarity, cleansing, and strength.

MAKE IT REAL!

To develop your solitude muscle, set aside a certain amount of time each day this week to sit alone in silence and listen to your own thoughts. Don't try to *do* anything. Just be, and listen. What do you notice?

Be still, and know that I am God
I will be exalted among the nations,
I will be exalted in the earth.
(Psalm 46:10)

THERE are some things you cannot know except through stillness. Like the glory of a flower, the calming music of the surf upon the sand, or the deep beauty of God's infinite power in your heart. We may be conscious of God while rushing about in our typical flurry of busyness and demands, but it is only as we willingly step into seasons of stillness and solitude that we truly come to understand who he is. He is not the sort of Art that can be known with a passing glance.

To know him truly requires a quiet space and attentive focus, a willingness to watch and listen until the revelation comes. "As the eyes of slaves look to the hand of their master, as the eyes of a maid look to the hand of her mistress, so our eyes look to the Lord our God, till he shows us his mercy" (Psalm 123:2). Some of his most beautiful gifts come only through stillness.

The stillness of solitude brings clarity to more than just our knowledge of God, however. It also awakens our awareness of our own hearts. And that is perhaps why we avoid it. We run from solitude to the degree that we run from ourselves. For solitude opens the window to your soul, and releases all that has been quietly sealed up and hidden away inside. We fear what might be there, lurking in the dark hidden by our busy lives— sorrow, loneliness, desperation, grief, weariness. But we do not understand that God's call to solitude is not a call to go off by yourself and face your struggles alone. It is the call to *come away with him*, so that he can minister to your soul and give you the healing gift of himself. "Come to me, all you who are weary and burdened, and I will give you rest. Take my yoke upon you and learn from me, for I am gentle and humble in heart, and you will find rest for your souls" (Matthew 11:28-29).

MAKE IT REAL!

As you get more accustomed to spending time alone in silence, begin to consciously welcome the Lord to join you in the stillness. Bring no agenda to your time with him other than to watch and listen for what he wants to reveal. Don't journal, and don't try to make anything happen. Just be available to him. After several silent encounters like this, take some time to journal your thoughts on the experience. What was the experience like for you? What is your reaction to it? What do you suppose God would want for you to do next?

THE CLEANSING OF SOLITUDE
Week 8—Wednesday

But Jesus often withdrew to lonely places and prayed.
(Luke 5:16)

WHAT was it that compelled Jesus to spend so much time alone? What was the hunger that drove him to solitude? Read through the Gospels and you will notice that on many occasions Jesus withdrew to lonely places when he was weary or when people began to press him to do or be something that was not true to who he was. (For examples, see Mark 6:31-46; Luke 6:11-12; and John 6:14-15.) We all need times of cleansing and refreshing—seasons in which we get away from the pressures and burdens that the world continually tries to lay upon our souls, and we reconnect with what is most true and real about who we are in the world and who God is in our lives.

I'm not talking merely about taking a vacation. Even a cursory glance at Jesus' example tells us that taking two weeks each year in the Bahamas or on the mountains of Colorado is not nearly enough to satisfy our souls' need for the cleansing and refreshment of solitude. For Christ, these solitary escapes were a regular and frequent part of his life. How much more, then, they should be for us. Surely the responsibilities of our lives are not more vitally important than his were. He was responsible for the salvation of the world! And yet he made the time for solitude, because he knew it was critical to the success of his calling and the life of his soul.

How would your life be different if you could escape from the world one full day out of each month and refresh your soul in solitude with God? What do you imagine would change? What would *have to* change to allow that time to happen?

Jesus has provided the example to follow. He has issued the invitation. What will it take for you to say yes?

MAKE IT REAL!

Pull out your calendar right now, and schedule a full day of
solitude sometime in the next month. Choose a place to go that is
away from the crowds, and lay plans for a full day with Jesus.
Read, meditate, pray, sing, journal, go for a hike—do whatever
your soul desires. But do it alone with him.

THE POWER OF SOLITUDE
Week 8—Thursday

And whenever Moses went out to the tent, all the people rose and stood at the entrances to their tents, watching Moses until he entered the tent. As Moses went into the tent, the pillar of cloud would come down and stay at the entrance, while the Lord spoke with Moses. Whenever the people saw the pillar of cloud standing at the entrance to the tent, they all stood and worshiped, each at the entrance to his tent. The Lord would speak to Moses face to face, as a man speaks with his friend.
(Exodus 33:8-11)

THE experience of purposeful solitude reconnects us with ourselves and our God. It brings clarity to our hearts and refreshment to our souls. Anyone who pursues solitude—even for a short season—will experience this. But for those who embrace the practice of solitude as a regular discipline in their lives, there is a deeper and more powerful gift to be received.

For those who make solitude a habit, the discipline becomes more than merely something you do. Solitude becomes a place you go—a sacred space set apart from the world and reserved for you and God alone. Like Moses in the Tent of Meeting, our solitude becomes a private, holy place of intimacy with God. And as with Moses, it brings not only clarity and refreshment to our souls—but also transformation and power.

The practice of regular solitude with God changes us. We come to know that we are loved in a way we never imagined. We see not only who he is and who we are, but also who we are becoming because of him. Through the mystical communion of solitude, we come to bear the power and love of God in our hearts and on our faces in a way that no other means can accomplish. Rather than using solitude as a means to escape the world, it becomes the means by which the Kingdom of God is brought *into* the world. For we become the vessels through which his power and glory are expressed.

MAKE IT REAL!

Are you ready for a deeper experience of God's love and power through the practice of solitude? Then begin your journey by reading the stories and insights of other believers who have traveled this path before you. Select one or more of the books from the "Book Recommendations" list, and begin reading it this month. Do it in private; tell no one but God. And be open to where the journey takes you.

BOOK RECOMMENDATIONS
A Search for Solitude 1952-1960 by Thomas Merton
Out of Solitude by Henri Nouwen
The Way of the Heart by Henri Nouwen

*But his delight is in the law of the Lord, and on his law he
meditates day and night. He is like a tree planted by streams of
water, which yields its fruit in season and whose leaf does not
wither. Whatever he does prospers.*
(Psalm 1:2-3)

WOULDN'T it be wonderful if—no matter what you
attempted in life, or what direction you chose to go—you were
guaranteed to prosper? Can you just imagine what that would be
like—to know that, regardless of how many obstacles you faced,
you would ultimately overcome them all? To be that strong,
resilient tree planted by streams of abundant water, whose leaf
never withers and whose fruit is always sweet? If you were living
that life, how would it differ from the life you're living today?
Who would you be then?

The truth is—that could be you. Really. The promise of God
is there for all of us. The water is waiting for you. All that's
lacking is a sincere, authentic decision to plant your heart firmly
beside the streams of God's powerful, transforming Word.

MAKE IT REAL!

How would you describe your current relationship with the
Bible? Are you on intimate terms with the Word? Does it
intimidate you? Does it bore you? Do you spend lots of free time
with it? Are you in love with it? Write a brief description of your
relationship with God's Word as it is right now. Then write a
description of the relationship with God's Word that you *wish*
you had. Make this wish your prayer for the coming month.

WEEKEND REFLECTION

TAKE a few moments this weekend to review the devotions you've read over this past week, as well as the "Make It Real!" steps you've done. As you reflect on the week, get curious about how God is moving in and through your life. Use these questions as a guide:

❖ What insights have you gained over the past week?
❖ What changes or shifts are you noticing in your relationship with God? with others? with yourself?
❖ What "Make It Real!" steps were the most meaningful for you? What made them meaningful?
❖ How will you live differently next week as a result of what you've learned?
❖ What support do you need to help you make that change?
❖ Based on your experiences over the past week, what do you most need from God right now?
❖ What do you suppose God might be wanting most from you right now?

CHALLENGE: If you missed one of the "Make It Real!" steps for this week, set aside time this weekend to complete it, and record your reactions, insights, and results in your journal.

For the word of God is living and active.
Sharper than any double-edged sword,
it penetrates even to dividing soul and spirit, joints and marrow;
it judges the thoughts and attitudes of the heart.
(Hebrews 4:12)

THE Word of God is a living force in the world. It has within it the power to perform what it proclaims. By that I mean, the Word carries the power to transform our hearts so that we become the supernatural people of God it calls us to be. But this transformation does not come merely from reading the Word, or even from the mental discipline of memorizing it—though both of these are fine habits to embrace. The power of transformation, however, comes from meditating on the Word.

Webster's defines *meditate* as "to engage in contemplation or reflection; to focus one's thoughts on; to reflect on or ponder over." This is a fair definition as far as it goes, but biblical meditation involves more than just engaging your mind. It also engages your heart, your feelings, and your will—in fact, your entire being. It means exposing your whole self to the scripture you are reading, and giving it the space and time it needs to delve into your spirit and search you out, until it has exposed and embraced all that is there, and lovingly transformed it into the image of Christ.

Imagine yourself lying in the sun on a beautiful beach somewhere in the Caribbean. You close your eyes and simply feel the impact of the sun upon your body. You open yourself to its rays and revel in the sensations of intense warmth and light that dance across your skin. You begin to sweat, and recognize that the sun is having an impact not only on your body, but also on your mind and heart. You accept this freely, and let the sun have its effect.

Biblical meditation is like that. It is sunbathing for the soul; and the Word of God is the sun.

MAKE IT REAL!

Make a list of your favorite verses, and read them aloud at least twice every morning before you get out of bed and every night before you go to sleep. Really listen to what the verses are saying. Do this for at least two weeks. When it's over, ask yourself: What did I notice? How has this experience impacted the way I'm engaging with life? with myself? with God?

Then you will know the truth, and the truth will set you free.
(John 8:32)

TO be truly free, you must come to know the truth. But the "knowing" Jesus speaks of here is not merely the intellectual sort. It goes far deeper than that. It's the sort of knowing you carry in your bones—the way you know the heart of your closest friend or the passion of your lover. It is intimate, unguarded, and fiercely real. Such knowledge can never come to you merely through observation or detached mental study. You must step in and partake of it directly.

Meditating on the Word is a means of partaking of God's transforming power—of literally taking it into our hearts the way we take nourishment into our bodies. As James describes it, it is receiving "the Word implanted, which is able to save your souls" (James 1:21, NASB). When we meditate on scripture, we focus not only on what it says, but also on the effect it has within us. For example, when you hear Jesus' proclamation that "the truth will set you free," what does that statement evoke in your spirit? What desire is awakened? What fear? What is the power you sense in the words? What does it want to accomplish in you? Meditating on scripture is like tasting fine wine. It is an extravagantly unhurried affair—one in which you remain purposefully present to each step of the exploration, paying attention not only to the wine of the Word, but also to its impact on your senses and the depth of your understanding.

When we meditate on the Word in this way, the Spirit of God is released to awaken us to its revelatory truth, and the Word itself comes to life within us. We find ourselves changed by its presence in a way that is as mysterious as it is wonderful. We meditate on Philippians 4:6, for example, and find over time that we are no longer burdened by anxiety the way we once were. Or we mediate on James 1:21 and find our hunger for the Word growing, expressing itself in ways we never expected. Through meditation, we begin to obey the commands of scripture, not from a sense of rote obligation, but through an inside-out transformation that we can explain only in terms of God's loving power at work in our lives. We are, quite simply, being redeemed by the power of the Word.

MAKE IT REAL!

Take a moment to connect with your heart. What do you really need to hear God say to you right now? Find one scripture passage that speaks to your need, and meditate on it one hour every day for the next week. Each day, write whatever new insights or questions that arise from the passage, no matter how insignificant they may seem. Also note how this passage impacts you. After a week, review what you've written and write what you've learned about yourself or about God through the experience.

Oh, how I love your law! I meditate on it all day long. Your commands make me wiser than my enemies, for they are ever with me. I have more insight than all my teachers, for I meditate on your statutes. I have more understanding than the elders, for I obey your precepts. I have kept my feet from every evil path so that I might obey your word. I have not departed from your laws, for you yourself have taught me. How sweet are your words to my taste, sweeter than honey to my mouth! I gain understanding from your precepts; therefore I hate every wrong path. Your word is a lamp to my feet and a light for my path.
(Psalm 119:97-105)

BIBLICAL meditation requires discipline and consistency. It is not the sort of thing you can do once in a while and expect that to do the trick. For its power to be fully known, meditation must become as vital to you as your food and drink. In fact, it must become so much a part of your life that it saturates the very atmosphere in which you live. God did not command Joshua to meditate on the Law once a week, or for a few minutes every other day. Rather he said, "Do not let this Book of the Law depart from your mouth; meditate on it day and night…" (Joshua 1:8). God commanded this because he knew there was no other way for Joshua to truly be transformed in heart and being—and thus, no other way for him to fulfill the great call God had placed on his life.

We are all Joshua. We will simply never become the men and women God has called us to be apart from the consistent discipline of meditating on the Word.

For those who embrace this discipline, however, the transformation it provokes speaks for itself. We are changed by the power of the Word, becoming literally who we were meant to be. We acquire wisdom, insight, and understanding. Life continues to bring its challenges, but we are never overcome. We abandon despair, for regardless of what happens, we know we will ultimately prosper. The Word of God becomes sweet to our souls, more beautiful that any beauty we have ever seen on earth, and more true than life itself. We fall in love, not only with the Word, but with the One who wrote it. And we discover, much to our delight, that that was the goal all along.

MAKE IT REAL!

For a more in-depth journey into discovering the value of biblical meditation, consider asking a few friends to join you in studying one of the books listed the "Book Recommendations" list. Discuss the book together and share how practicing regular biblical meditation impacts who you are and how you live.

BOOK RECOMMENDATIONS
Meditating on the Word by Dietrich Bonhoeffer
Contemplative Bible Reading: Experiencing God Through Scripture, Spiritual Formation Study Guide by Richard Peace
Study and Meditation, Spiritual Disciplines Bible Study by Jan Johnson

*Therefore I tell you, whatever you ask for in prayer,
believe that you have received it, and it will be yours.*
(Mark 11:24)

IMAGINE that the President of the United States showed up at
your doorstep holding a beautifully wrapped gift. As he hands it
to you, he says, "In this box is a special telephone. Just plug it in,
and you'll have a direct line to me 24/7. You see, although I am
the president, I've also taken it upon myself to be your personal
advocate. Anytime you have a need or question or just want to
talk, just pick up the phone and I'll be there. I promise to bring all
the power and authority of my office to bear toward solving any
dilemma you face and to help you succeed in every arena of your
life. All I ask is that you use it regularly, and have faith in my
promise to help you."

Of course, such a scene is not likely to happen to any us in
this lifetime. But if it did, who among us would turn down such a
generous offer? Not me, that's for sure. And probably not you.
For we all know that having that kind of direct access to the
President would change our lives overnight.

Even so, it's pretty telling that we can feel more excitement
over a crazy idea like this than we do when we come to pray to
God—even though God sits far above the President in power and
authority; he loves us far more than the President ever could; and
prayer is far more intimate and direct than a telephone call. When
you look at it that way, it's a wonder that we have to be
commanded to pray at all.

And it begs the question: What are we really believing about
prayer?

MAKE IT REAL!

What do you really believe about prayer? Try this simple exercise to find out. In your journal, make a list of personal belief statements regarding prayer. Simply begin each statement with something like this: "I believe that my prayers…"; "When I pray…"; or "For me, prayer is…" Then complete the statements with whatever comes to mind. Don't try to edit your thoughts too much at first. When the list feels complete, go back through and read what you wrote. What do these gut-level responses tell you about your beliefs around prayer?

But when you pray, go into your room, close the door and pray to your Father, who is unseen. Then your Father, who sees what is done in secret, will reward you.
(Matthew 6:6)

PRAYER is the heart and soul of our love affair with God. It is the place of divine communion—of seeing and being seen; of hearing and being heard; of loving and being loved. Prayer is the catalyst that unleashes God's infinite power into our lives. And yet for all that, it is a stunningly simple act. All it requires is an open heart, open ears, and faith. It is, in fact, the simplicity of prayer that tempts us to be suspicious of it. Surely connecting with the God of the universe cannot be so simple. He can't really be listening to me, can he? I am only one voice among billions.

And yet, he does. He's listening to you even now as you read this. Ready to hear every question, every dream, every pain you're holding in your heart, even those you never share with anyone else. His love for you is so complete, so utterly full and indomitable, that he made certain that prayer left no barriers between his heart and yours. Prayer is simple because God loves you. But don't mistake that to mean that prayer is not powerful.

We've often heard it said that prayer is simply talking to God. But that's a paltry definition. For prayer is also listening to God, singing with God, dancing with God, playing with God, laughing with God, learning from God, and a hundred other things you would naturally do with the Lover of your Soul. Prayer is the atmosphere in which your true heart comes alive.

Someone once said that no one can stand long in God's presence and not be changed. That comes closer to defining the truth and mystery of prayer. For prayer—simple prayer—is the place where we are transformed.

MAKE IT REAL!

If you had the prayer life you really wanted, what would it look like? In your journal, write a description of it. Then take your description to God, and make *that* the focus of your prayers for the next month.

TAKE a few moments this weekend to review the devotions you've read over this past week, as well as the "Make It Real!" steps you've done. As you reflect on the week, get curious about how God is moving in and through your life. Use these questions as a guide:

- ❖ What insights have you gained over the past week?
- ❖ What changes or shifts are you noticing in your relationship with God? with others? with yourself?
- ❖ What "Make It Real!" steps were the most meaningful for you? What made them meaningful?
- ❖ How will you live differently next week as a result of what you've learned?
- ❖ What support do you need to help you make that change?
- ❖ Based on your experiences over the past week, what do you most need from God right now?
- ❖ What do you suppose God might be wanting most from you right now?

CHALLENGE: If you missed one of the "Make It Real!" steps for this week, set aside time this weekend to complete it, and record your reactions, insights, and results in your journal.

DEVOTION AND DISCIPLINE
Week 10—Monday

Devote yourselves to prayer, being watchful and thankful.
(Colossians 4:2)

FOR any relationship to flourish, regular, open communication is key. We know this from experience. Suppose you had a "best" friend who spoke to you, on average, once each week. In each conversation he or she thanked you for your friendship, complained a while about all the problems he or she was facing, then promptly handed you a list of personal requests and walked away. You wouldn't want to have a friend like that for long. And yet we wonder why our prayer life often feels so flat and void of life.

Prayer *is* relationship. And devotion to prayer involves far more than delivering a weekly (or daily) wish list to God. Not that God doesn't want to hear your requests. Of course he does— and he will answer them. But the ultimate goal of prayer is not merely to get something *from* God; rather, it is to develop something *with* God. With relationship as the goal, prayer becomes an invitation to share your joys and your dreams with the Creator of your soul, and to ask him to do the same with you.

Such unguarded honesty does not come easily for most of us—even with Someone as trustworthy as God. It requires a disciplined commitment to keep the channels of communication open, and a heart-fueled devotion to the intimacy of the relationship.

If your heart were totally unguarded right now, what would it really want to say to God? What would it want to know about him? Begin your devotion there. With practice and consistency in the place of honesty, you will soon find there's more to prayer than you imagined.

MAKE IT REAL!

When you are totally unguarded, who are you? When you look at your relationship with God from that place, what do you see? What do you really want God to know about you? What do you really want to know about him? From that unguarded place, create a list of items to share and questions to ask in your prayer time with God. Then patiently address each one in turn, all the while keeping your focus not on getting answers, but on deepening your relationship with God.

PARTNERSHIP AND POWER
Week 10—Tuesday

And pray in the Spirit on all occasions
with all kinds of prayers and requests.
With this in mind, be alert and always keep on praying
for all the saints.
(Ephesians 6:18)

ONCE you've settled into the mystery and discipline of prayer, unusual things begin to happen. The Spirit of God begins to whisper to your heart, not about you, but about his work in the world. He tells you about his heart for your neighbor, or for that co-worker of yours who always looks so sad. He tells you about his desire for your city, or for your nation, or for some nation halfway across the world.

When these whisperings first begin, we often don't know what to do with them. "Is that God?" we ask, unsure. "Why is he telling me this? Am I supposed to do something? But what can I do?" Most of the time, the only thing he's asking you to do is share his burden with him, and pray. But sometimes the revelation comes with a request for you to act. Perhaps he wants you to share love with someone he cares about—by giving a gift, lending your assistance in some practical way, or passing on a special message he's given you to share. Or perhaps he wants you to leave your home to bring his light to a people in some other land. Whatever it is, you will know it.

When this begins to happen to you, rejoice! For it is a sign that God feels confident enough in your relationship to trust you with his secrets. Your relationship has grown from one of servant/master to one of friendship. As Jesus said to his disciples, "I no longer call you servants, because a servant does not know his master's business. Instead, I have called you friends, for everything that I learned from my Father I have made known to you" (John 15:15).

As you move forward in the discipline of prayer, you will experience profound personal transformation. You will develop a thriving, communicative relationship with God. But in time, you will also become God's friend—and that is a partnership of great power. Your prayers become a catalyst for adventure and purpose—as God invites you to join him where he is, and do with him what he is doing in the world.

MAKE IT REAL!

Invite a few of your closest Christian allies to join you in deepening the discipline of prayer in your life. You might use a book on prayer to guide your quest (*Prayer* by Richard Foster is one excellent choice, but there are many others). You might consider organizing a prayer retreat together, or joining one of the many national prayer organizations that focus on national or international concerns. Or you might simply begin with a biblical word study on "prayer." After you complete each project, get together and discuss how God has moved in your lives, and ask him what he wants for your group to do next.

THE PARADOX OF WEAKNESS
Week 10—Wednesday

Do you not know? Have you not heard? The Everlasting God, the Lord, the Creator of the ends of the earth does not become weary or tired. His understanding is inscrutable. He gives strength to the weary, and to him who lacks might He increases power.
(Isaiah 40:28-29, NASB)

IN our journey as followers of God, he never tells us that we will not grow weary. He never says to us, "Your heart will never fail." He knows that it will. What he tells us instead is that *his* heart, *his* strength is endless and unwavering. He—the Lord—can never grow tired. His great strength is unaffected by any trial. It is inexhaustible and everlasting.

This is good to remember in those times when the burden of your life becomes too great for your heart; when the world comes closing in and whatever fire was once burning in your soul for life and for God seems reduced to nothing but ashes; when the only cry you can muster is a silent stare toward heaven because you've lost even the strength of your voice to pray anymore. In those times, let this be your anchor: No matter how great my difficulty, no matter how exhausted my soul has become, my God remains strong and true. There is no end to his reserves. *And he has promised to give me himself.*

MAKE IT REAL!

When are you weakest in life? What are the burdens that make you feel that way? In your journal, list your burdens and your weaknesses. If you showed this list to your closest friends, what would it tell them about you? If you showed it to God, what are you afraid he might say? What do you wish he would say?

THE GIFT OF BEING WEAK
Week 10—Thursday

Whom have I in heaven but You? And besides You, I desire
nothing on earth. My flesh and my heart may fail, but God is the
strength of my heart and my portion forever.
(Psalm 73:25-26, NASB)

THE Lord will never make us strong in ourselves—that is, in our
human ability; that is not his aim as our Redeemer. Instead, his
purpose is to become our Strength. And it is only in those times
when we are weakest, when our hearts fail and our spirits grow
weary, that we can truly understand this. For only when we come
to the end of ourselves do we see the absurdity of ever believing
we could be strong in the first place. In weakness, we see
ourselves more clearly. And we see God more clearly as well.

When you are overcome by life, it does no good to beg God
to make you strong. Rather, when you've come to end of
yourself, you have only one true recourse in Christ: To step into
him, cover yourself with him, abandon yourself to him, let go of
your striving and your thinking and your worry and everything
that lures you to rely on yourself, and invite him to be Strength in
you.

This is not an exchange—that is, it is not a swapping of your
weakness for his strength. Rather, it is an intimate union. It is a
stepping into his power and letting go of your own. It is his
Strength in your weakness—not instead of, but *in*. Your
weakness remains, only now it is embraced in God's strength.

It is this communion—this union of the weak with the
Strong—that the Apostle Paul speaks of 2 Corinthians 12:9-10:
"But he said to me, 'My grace is sufficient for you, for my power
is made perfect in weakness.' Therefore I will boast all the more
gladly about my weaknesses, so that Christ's power may rest on
me. That is why, for Christ's sake, I delight in weaknesses, in
insults, in hardships, in persecutions, in difficulties. For when I
am weak, then I am strong."

When you choose Paul's perspective for yourself, then you no longer see your weaknesses as a burden. Instead, they become a doorway to intimacy with God.

MAKE IT REAL!

When you need strength in life, where do you go to find it? What do you do to get it? In your journal, write a series of statements about your own search for strength. Begin each one this way: "When I feel weak or burdened, I try to get strength by…" Once you've finished, read through your statements. Notice where God is in the mix. Notice where he's not. Based on what you've written, what would you say you really believe about your capacity to be strong in yourself? about God's capacity to be strong in you?

Then Jesus said, "Come to me, all of you who are weary and carry heavy burdens, and I will give you rest. Take my yoke upon you. Let me teach you, because I am humble and gentle, and you will find rest for your souls. For my yoke fits perfectly, and the burden I give you is light."
(Matthew 11:28-30, NLT)

REMEMBER this: It is not the strong that Jesus calls to himself, but the weak. So when your world has overwhelmed you, and the burdens upon you have become too much to bear, take heart in this: You are the very one Jesus is looking for. You are the one he calls to and hopes will come. You are the one he wants to love.

But when you do come to Jesus, do not think it will be enough to simply hold up your weakness or your burden and ask for God's help. He's asking more of you than that. He's asking you to truly lay your burden down—which is a profound act of radical faith. You must relinquish your burden altogether. You must stop fretting over it, stop demanding he do something about it, stop *even looking at it*—and turn your eyes on Jesus exclusively. Only then will you come to understand that the deeper story of your life was never really about your burden to begin with; rather, it is about the intimate relationship between you and God.

It always has been.

"Take my yoke upon you. Let me teach you…" Once you have laid down your burden and abandoned your heart to his strength, he will ask you to take on his yoke—that is, the yoke of discipleship. He will become your teacher—but his teaching will not be what you expect. For instead of teaching you about mastering your weakness or how you can shoulder the burden next time on your own, Jesus will begin to teach you about *himself.* He will reveal to you who he is.

And if you truly listen, and truly learn, you will soon discover that *knowing him* is the strength and victory you were looking for all along.

MAKE IT REAL!

What are the burdens you've never really given to Jesus (you know—the areas of weakness or personal struggle that continue to weigh on your heart no matter how often you "give" them to God)? What do you imagine it would take for you to really, finally let it go? Talk to a trusted friend or two about your burden. Ask them to share what they think might be keeping you from totally giving it over to Jesus. Then make the decision to do whatever it takes to commit it to God once and for all.

TAKE a few moments this weekend to review the devotions you've read over this past week, as well as the "Make It Real!" steps you've done. As you reflect on the week, get curious about how God is moving in and through your life. Use these questions as a guide:

❖ What insights have you gained over the past week?
❖ What changes or shifts are you noticing in your relationship with God? with others? with yourself?
❖ What "Make It Real!" steps were the most meaningful for you? What made them meaningful?
❖ How will you live differently next week as a result of what you've learned?
❖ What support do you need to help you make that change?
❖ Based on your experiences over the past week, what do you most need from God right now?
❖ What do you suppose God might be wanting most from you right now?

CHALLENGE: If you missed one of the "Make It Real!" steps for this week, set aside time this weekend to complete it, and record your reactions, insights, and results in your journal.

THE STRONG IN GOD
Week 11—Monday

Blessed are those whose strength is in you, who have set their hearts on pilgrimage. As they pass through the Valley of Baca, they make it a place of springs; the autumn rains also cover it with pools. They go from strength to strength, till each appears before God in Zion.
(Psalm 84:5-7)

THE Strong in God are marked by these three qualities:
- their hearts are set on following God above all other loves and desires;
- their strength (really God's strength *in them*) grows stronger through each season they face; and
- they become catalysts of blessing and transformation everywhere they go.

This is the heritage of the weak who make God their Strength: They become God's agents of power and transformation in the world. This does not mean they are not still weak—for they most certainly are, and they know it to their very core. But they have made the profound decision to accept their weakness for what it is, to not despise it, and to utterly surrender it to God. So he becomes Strength in them.

You know these Christians by their effect on you and their impact on the world around them. You feel drawn to them in the same way the thirsty are drawn to water. Their very presence, and especially their words, quench your soul, encourage your heart, and renew your capacity to believe. The wake of their lives is littered with stories of blessing, encouragement, and transformed hearts. You get the sense that they know a secret about abundance in life, and you continually feel pulled toward them to find out what it is.

But the secret is really laid open right in front of you. "For who is God besides the Lord? And who is the Rock except our God? It is God who arms me with strength and makes my way perfect. He makes my feet like the feet of a deer; he enables me to stand on the heights. He trains my hands for battle; my arms can bend a bow of bronze" (Psalm 18:31-34).

The secret of the Strong in God is that they know they are weak, but that their weakness no longer matters to them. What matters to them is that *God* is strong—for they know that so long as their strength is in him, they cannot be overcome.

MAKE IT REAL!

Look back at the list of weaknesses you created earlier. How would your life be different if you believed all these weaknesses were actually gifts—portals through which you can experience God's profound strength in your life? For the next few weeks, select one weakness you particularly dislike and practice giving it over to God each day. Ask God to reveal himself to you *through that weakness*. Every day or two, record your impressions in your journal. Then at the end of two weeks, notice the change in your relationship with God, and your effect on the people around you.

THE DISCIPLINE OF WORSHIP
Week 11—Tuesday

Worship the Lord in holy attire; tremble before Him, all the earth.
(Psalm 96:9, NASB)

WHAT is it to worship God? Is it singing a song? Is it giving him money, attending a church service, or serving the poor in his name? Is it living a "righteous" life, doing your best to remain free of the entanglements that come from wanting to possess or control the passing attractions of this world? The answer is: No. None of these activities in themselves are worship. For they are all outward displays of something deeper, something less tangible, yet far more real than any outward action or ritual. You can build a church brick by brick with your bare hands and call it worship, but if your heart is more focused on gaining glory for yourself than on giving glory to God, then your great sacrifice is anything but worship.

At least, it is not worship of God.

Worship is not defined by a particular act, but rather by the heart attitude of the person doing the acting. It is like a garment we wear over our hearts—our "holy attire," as the psalmist describes it. Once the garment is donned, then every act—from feeding the poor to ironing your clothes—becomes worship.

So what is the garment of worship? What are the attributes of this "holy attire" that God calls us to wear? It is a garment woven not primarily of actions, but of deep and disciplined attitudes. Of these deep disciplines, three stand out as key to the worshipper's heart: the discipline of gratitude, the discipline of intimate humility, and the discipline of celebration.

MAKE IT REAL!

For the next few days, ponder this question in your heart: "What is it to worship God?" Ask God to speak to you about this question, and guide you toward an answer through his Word, through his Spirit, through people or through any other means he wishes. At the end of the week, journal your insights.

THE DISCIPLINE OF GRATITUDE
Week 11—Wednesday

Give thanks to the Lord, call on his name;
make known among the nations what he has done.
(1 Chronicles 16:8)

A grateful heart is not something we gain by chance. It is not
some lucky byproduct of winning the lottery or finding your soul
mate or getting a promotion at work. Those events may make us
feel grateful for a time. But the practice of gratitude, as a
lifestyle, is a choice that comes from a place far deeper than mere
circumstance can reach. It is a decision—a disciplined ongoing
choice—to live gratefully before God, regardless of whether you
win the lottery, land the promotion, or find your true love. It is a
discipline not merely of action, but of *how we see the world.* In
choosing a lifestyle of gratitude, we consciously place our heart's
focus on life's myriad gifts more than its costs—from the grace
to draw breath to the sweet taste of food to the laughter of
children and the beauty of the sky. We speak our thanks in every
circumstance. We choose joy. And we believe in God's good
heart, even when life is hard.

In fact, it is during those seasons when life seems hardest—
when we lose the job or are forced to walk away from yet another
failed relationship—that the true beauty and power of a grateful
heart is revealed. For it is only in those situations that we realize
that the gifts of this world, however wonderful they may be,
cannot compare to the deeper, eternal gift we already possess, a
gift which no circumstance has the power to take away. As the
prophet Habakkuk proclaims:

"Though the fig tree does not bud and there are no grapes on
the vines, though the olive crop fails and the fields produce no
food, though there are no sheep in the pen and no cattle in the
stalls, yet I will rejoice in the Lord, I will be joyful in God my
Savior. The Sovereign Lord is my strength; he makes my feet like
the feet of a deer, he enables me to go on the heights" (Habakkuk
3:17-19).

The discipline of gratitude keeps us mindful of where our true happiness and joy resides—not in circumstance, but in Christ alone.

MAKE IT REAL!

This week, try this experiment in gratitude: Go off by yourself with journal and pen, and spend some time writing down *everything* you are thankful for. Keep going until you run out of things to write. When you finish, read through your list. What do you notice? What does the list tell you about yourself? about the level of gratitude in your life?

THE DISCIPLINE OF INTIMATE HUMILITY
Week 11—Thursday

Whom have I in heaven but you? And earth has nothing I desire besides you. My flesh and my heart may fail, but God is the strength of my heart and my portion forever. Those who are far from you will perish; you destroy all who are unfaithful to you. But as for me, it is good to be near God. I have made the Sovereign Lord my refuge; I will tell of all your deeds.
(Psalm 73:25-28)

WORSHIP, when it's real, is naked. It is desperate and honest and anything but eloquent. In true worship, there is no pretense before God, no performance, no hiding of flaws. It is the place where all the walls you have built finally crumble and dissolve— until there is only you, alone, standing in the consuming fire of God's holy presence. And yet, like the burning bush on Sinai, you are not consumed—and you realize, as Moses did, that the only reason you are alive is because you are loved.

It is the blood of Christ that allows this miracle to happen every time we come before God. But until you make the conscious choice to open your heart to God in intimate humility, you will never truly experience it.

As with other disciplines of worship, intimate humility is not so much a specific action or ritual as it is a way of *being* with God. It is the choice to live naked before God—unguarded, brutally honest, keenly aware that you are nothing without him, and yet equally convinced that you are loved. In worship, intimate humility is the place of sacrifice and surrender. It is the place of fasting and tears and the sharing of secrets, but it is also the place of transformation. For only in intimate humility do we truly forget about ourselves—our nakedness, our barrenness, our fear, weakness and doubt—and focus our full attention on him. Only later do we realize that this act of abandoned surrender is actually the instrument by which we are changed. As Paul affirms, "But we all, with unveiled face, beholding as in a mirror the glory of the Lord, are being transformed into the same image from glory to glory, just as from the Lord, the Spirit" (2 Corinthians 3:18, NASB).

MAKE IT REAL!

What are the walls that you're currently hiding behind in your life? What is it you're trying to protect? What is it that you don't want anyone to see? I challenge you to choose one person—a mature Christian and someone you trust—and share with him or her the things you've been hiding. Then ask your friend to join you in going to God in intimate humility and, together, letting all the walls fall down before him.

THE DISCIPLINE OF CELEBRATION
Week 11—Friday

Rejoice in the Lord always. I will say it again: Rejoice!
(Philippians 4:4)

IT is a travesty that the worship in our churches is so often restricted to somber ritual. We bow our heads to ponder God, and sing our songs of devotion in quiet reflective tones, being ever mindful of the grave seriousness of approaching the throne of the Almighty. While such obeisance can most certainly be worshipful, it is not the sum of all that worship can or must be. For worship is also free-spirited giddiness and delight. It is raucous laughter, unbridled rejoicing, feasting, and dance. It is reveling in God's goodness, and celebrating the life and salvation he has given. To hold a party in celebration of God's goodness in our lives is every bit as much worship as the fasting and prayer of solitude. And *both* have a place in the life of every believer.

Celebration is central to the Christian experience. It is a key evidence of God's Spirit in our lives and a testimony to the world of the joy that comes from walking with Jesus and enjoying his salvation. For this very reason, it is also one of the key areas of our lives that our enemy strives to undermine and destroy. There is nothing quite so dismal and pathetic as a joyless Christian— and few things are more damaging to the spread of the gospel. Our enemy knows this and will do everything in his power to turn you into one.

That is in part why God's Word commands us to celebrate. We must be regularly reminded to look beyond the struggles of the moment, and see the outcome that has already been written. The battle that has already been won. The discipline of regular celebration brings that reminder to our hearts, and reopens the door of invitation from Jesus—to dance in the midst of him through the circumstances of this life, and to let our hearts come alive with laughter and song for the salvation and joy we have found in him.

MAKE IT REAL!

When was the last time you celebrated your salvation in Christ? Well, that's too long! This month, gather some friends and organize a big party to celebrate Christ's presence and work in your lives. Include music, dancing, feasting, games, and sharing stories of God's work in your lives—anything that feels good to your soul and honoring to God.

WEEKEND REFLECTION

TAKE a few moments this weekend to review the devotions you've read over this past week, as well as the "Make It Real!" steps you've done. As you reflect on the week, get curious about how God is moving in and through your life. Use these questions as a guide:

- ❖ What insights have you gained over the past week?
- ❖ What changes or shifts are you noticing in your relationship with God? with others? with yourself?
- ❖ What "Make It Real!" steps were the most meaningful for you? What made them meaningful?
- ❖ How will you live differently next week as a result of what you've learned?
- ❖ What support do you need to help you make that change?
- ❖ Based on your experiences over the past week, what do you most need from God right now?
- ❖ What do you suppose God might be wanting most from you right now?

CHALLENGE: If you missed one of the "Make It Real!" steps for this week, set aside time this weekend to complete it, and record your reactions, insights, and results in your journal.

When the people saw the thunder and lightning and heard the
trumpet and saw the mountain in smoke, they trembled with fear.
They stayed at a distance and said to Moses, "Speak to us
yourself and we will listen. But do not have God speak to us or
we will die."
(Exodus 20:18-19)

THE people of Israel followed God through the desert for 40
years. But even after all that God had done in that time to
demonstrate his love and draw them to himself, the half-
heartedness of their devotion remained unchanged. They
followed him, but did not truly want to know him. They followed
him, but did not want to see him unveiled. They loved the God In
The Distance—the one who dwelt on the horizon in the pillar of
cloud and fire, or concealed himself within the confines of a tent
where only Moses would go. They wanted him present, but they
did not want him close. Certainly they did not want to hear his
voice for themselves, or see his face, for they knew quite rightly
that to see God as he truly is meant that they would have to die.
And they simply loved themselves too much for that.

But Moses was not like them. He went where none of them
would go, and listened to what none of them would hear. He
braved the holy mountain, not just out of obligation to his people,
but more from his own desire. For above all else, Moses longed
to see the face of God.

To delve into the study of God's Word is like choosing to
climb Mount Sinai on that day when Israel backed away. For like
that mountain, we know that the unveiled glory of God rests in
the heights and hidden places of his Word, cloaked in a mystery
not unlike the clouds that shrouded Sinai's peak. Those who
undertake such a journey do not do so merely because they are
commanded. Rather, they are those with hearts like Moses'—
willing to lay down their lives to know God face to face.

MAKE IT REAL!

When it comes to encountering God, how close is too close for you? Read through the story of the Israelites in Exodus 20, and put yourself into the narrative. If you were a part of the story, where would you have stood when God showed up on the mountain? Would you have stayed at the base or gone up the slope? Would you have braved the peak itself? Or would you have shied away from the mountain? What does your response say about how close you want God to be in your life today?

The unfolding of your words gives light
it gives understanding to the simple.
(Psalm 119:130)

THE journey to understanding the Word of God, though not easy, is delightful and full of treasure. It is the treasure of it all, in fact, that inspires us to go on. Upturning every word, unpacking every phrase reveals a deeper and richer hue of God's truth and love than we had seen before. The Word of God is infinitely deep. There is no end to its unfolding.

That is not to say that the truth of the Word is ever defined by the beholder. For no one who sincerely studies the Word of God defines his learning by what he wants the Word to say or by what he feels like it is saying. Rather, he studies the Word without presumption or prejudice to discover exactly what it actually says—unfiltered and full of challenge. This is especially difficult for those who, having grown up in the church, may have been indoctrinated to draw simplistic, tired conclusions from familiar passages or stories. We must unlearn these things, or at least consciously suspend them, before we can discover what is honestly being revealed.

One of the biggest misconceptions about the Word of God is that it is primarily an Answer Book—something like a dictionary or encyclopedia for right living. Though there are answers within it, the Word is not merely that. Nor is it merely a book of rules or lectures. Neither is it just a book of formulas to be deciphered. Any attempt to study the Word through these limited lenses may make you smart, and will certainly make you religious, but it will not bring you life.

The Word is primarily a book of stories whose collective singular purpose is to reveal the Storyteller. He is the central character on every page—even those that may seem on the surface to be about other things. Once you understand that, then the study of the Word ceases to be a quest for facts and rules and pat answers to real problems, and instead becomes what it is meant to be: a journey to authentic, real relationship with God.

MAKE IT REAL!

When you think of "Bible study," what do you feel? What images does it evoke? What do you expect to get out of it, if anything? Set some time aside this week to explore your own perspective on studying God's Word. Record your insights in your journal, then invite a friend to discuss them with you. Prayerfully ask each other, "What's really true about your perspective on Bible study? What's not true? What needs to happen in you for Bible study to become a deeper, more consistent discipline in your life?"

SHATTERED, REFINED AND REFORGED
Week 12—Wednesday

"Is not my word like fire," declares the Lord,
"and like a hammer that breaks a rock in pieces?"
(Jeremiah 23:29)

LIKE all things that come from God, his Word is both absolutely true and infinitely powerful—and therefore, it is utterly dangerous. Often, we try to mitigate the danger of the Word, perhaps even inoculate ourselves against it, by reducing its message or its stories to simplistic platitudes or principles that neither threaten us nor require us to engage with Mystery. But once you truly begin to study the Word, all such pretensions soon fall away. For the Word itself will gradually unravel and collapse any safe or convenient preconceptions you hold regarding who God is or what it means to know and follow him.

The study of the Word shatters paradigms. It shakes your foundations—demolishing all your pretensions and leaving only that which is utterly true and real within your heart. After the shaking, it refines what remains, reinforcing it by the power of the life unleashed through its redeeming truth.

The genuine study of the Word will, quite simply, remake you. It will awaken your desire—not for knowledge, but for relationship. You will eventually find you can no longer tolerate distance between you and God—and realize with surprise and delight that this was his purpose all along.

MAKE IT REAL!

If you're not already part of a regular Bible study group, join one. When you do, however, make sure that the group's primary focus is actually "Bible study" and not "fellowship" or "social action" or some other emphasis. Although these other types of groups are good and can be a wonderful encouragement in your walk with Christ, they should not be confused with a true Bible study group, whose emphasis is clearly on delving into the disciplined study of God's Word.

THE TRANSFORMED HEART · 125

THE SWORD WE WIELD
Week 12—Thursday

Do your best to present yourself to God as one approved,
a workman who does not need to be ashamed
and who correctly handles the word of truth.
(2 Timothy 2:15)

THE study of the Word is a journey God invites us all to take. God uses this journey to reshape your heart, awaken your understanding, and guide you into authentic relationship with him as he truly is. But that journey also requires something of you. It is simply not enough to say, "I want to study God's Word more." You must move your heart beyond wishing to choice. Will you commit yourself to the habit of Bible study as a holy discipline— one that requires your preparation, dedication and consistency? Your desire to study is good, but beware of fooling yourself into believing that your good intention alone is enough to please God. In the end, it is what you do with that intention that reveals your true heart.

There are at least a dozen or more widely-acclaimed dynamic methods for studying the Word. Explore them. Learn them. Let them serve as guides in your journey to know God. But let nothing deter you from your calling to be a student of the Word. The treasures awaiting you in its pages are not only for you, but also for the world *through you*. It is for good reason that the Word is called a sword, for in the right hands it becomes a powerful weapon both to cripple the enemy and to free the captive heart. But how can you effectively wield it in battle unless you have first learned to wield it in the private chambers of your soul? The warrior who flippantly handles his sword is at best a fool, and at worst, a danger to all who cross his path.

MAKE IT REAL!

To take your personal Bible study discipline to the next level—go to your local library or bookstore and check out one or more of the books listed in the "Book Recommendations" list. Use them as guidebooks in exploring the various methods for studying God's Word.

BOOK RECOMMENDATIONS
How to Study Your Bible by Kay Arthur
Discipleship Journal's Best Bible Study Methods by NavPress
How to Read the Bible for All It's Worth by Gordon D. Fee &
     Douglas Stuart

THE LOST ART OF FASTING
Week 12—Friday

*When you fast, do not look somber as the hypocrites do, for they
disfigure their faces to show men they are fasting. I tell you the
truth, they have received their reward in full. But when you fast,
put oil on your head and wash your face, so that it will not be
obvious to men that you are fasting, but only to your Father, who
is unseen; and your Father, who sees what is done in secret, will
reward you.*
(Matthew 6:16-18)

JESUS cautioned us never to make a public show of fasting.
When it's sincere, fasting is a deeply personal act—closely bound
up in the private intimacy between you and God. We may share
our decision to fast with a few of those closest to us to garner
their support or ask them to fast in concert with us, but for the
most part fasting is a choice best kept to yourself.

Sadly, however, many Christians have used Jesus' command
to fast in private as a loophole to abandon the practice altogether.
This is a serious error in judgment—but even more, it says
something alarming about the condition of our hearts. Why have
so many of us discarded this ancient hallowed practice from our
lives?

Certainly, for Christians, fasting is not an issue of the law as
it was for the Israelites. In Christ, we are free to choose whether
and when we want to include it in our lives. But it is still an issue
of the heart. What does it say about our desire for God, our
hunger for his presence, and our passion for his will that we fast
so little in seeking him?

And yet, perhaps it is not only our hearts, but also our lack of
understanding that makes fasting seem so archaic and strange to
our sensibilities. After all, what does fasting really accomplish in
the end? And how can such a practice practically fit into the busy
life of the postmodern world?

"Let us examine our ways and test them," cries the prophet
Jeremiah, "and let us return to the Lord" (Lamentations 3:40).
Perhaps it's time we examined our ways with respect to fasting,

so that we might come to the Lord with fresh hearts and a renewed understanding of what it means to seek him with our whole being.

MAKE IT REAL!

Set aside some time this week to search through God's Word for verses and stories related to fasting. Record your insights in your journal.

WEEKEND REFLECTION

TAKE a few moments this weekend to review the devotions you've read over this past week, as well as the "Make It Real!" steps you've done. As you reflect on the week, get curious about how God is moving in and through your life. Use these questions as a guide:

- ❖ What insights have you gained over the past week?
- ❖ What changes or shifts are you noticing in your relationship with God? with others? with yourself?
- ❖ What "Make It Real!" steps were the most meaningful for you? What made them meaningful?
- ❖ How will you live differently next week as a result of what you've learned?
- ❖ What support do you need to help you make that change?
- ❖ Based on your experiences over the past week, what do you most need from God right now?
- ❖ What do you suppose God might be wanting most from you right now?

CHALLENGE: If you missed one of the "Make It Real!" steps for this week, set aside time this weekend to complete it, and record your reactions, insights, and results in your journal.

*"Even now," declares the Lord, "return to me with all your
heart, with fasting and weeping and mourning. Rend your heart
and not your garments. Return to the Lord your God, for he is
gracious and compassionate, slow to anger and abounding in
love, and he relents from sending calamity."*
(Joel 2:12-13)

THE logistics of a biblical fast vary by circumstance in scripture.
Sometimes it was a 24-hour day void of food or drink. Other
times it was a longer period, but the fast was observed only from
dawn to dusk. And yet, whatever the form, the cry of the human
heart to reconnect with God was always central to its purpose.

Fasting, by its nature, awakens us to repentance. It reconnects
us to our utter inability to live without the sustaining blessings of
God. It humbles us to remember that we are not, after all, the
self-sufficient lords of our own lives. But most importantly, it
refocuses our hearts to see what we truly need for genuine life in
this world, and to recognize where we have wasted our energy on
the frivolous and profane.

Ultimately, this is not a fast we do for God's benefit, but
rather for our own. We cry out as David did, "Search me, O God,
and know my heart"; so we, in turn, do the same. We fast to
search our own souls in tandem with Christ. Without the
distracting crutches of creature comforts, and with an ever-
increasing awareness of our need, we look within, holding in our
spirits this singular purpose: to uproot and toss aside anything he
finds within us that is not pleasing to him.

MAKE IT REAL!

Make a list of any attitudes, choices, or behaviors in your life that you suspect may be keeping you from following Jesus with your whole heart. Then set aside one or two days this week to fast and seek God's perspective on the items you listed. As you fast, notice what attitudes and thoughts rise up in you. What are they telling you about your own heart? about your relationship with God?

THE FAST OF SUPPLICATION
Week 13—Tuesday

So I turned to the Lord God and pleaded with him
in prayer and petition, in fasting,
and in sackcloth and ashes.
(Daniel 9:3)

THERE comes a time in everyone's life when the only thing left in you to do is collapse on the ground in desperation and plead with God. The world is too much for all of us. It is unfair, and frequently deals us blows to shatter our souls without reason or cause. It does not care that your heart is breaking or that your strength is spent. Indeed, sometimes it doesn't even notice you are there.

But God does. He sees us all, and listens to our every passing thought with love and captive interest. And it is precisely for that reason that we choose, in faith, to seek him through fasting and prayer.

The fast of supplication is the fast of Daniel to see his nation delivered from captivity. It is the fast of David to save the life of his infant son. It is the fast of Esther to deliver her people from certain destruction. And it is the fast that you will choose—in that moment when you recognize your own powerlessness and turn your heart to seek God's intervening strength.

The fast of supplication is the fast of longing, of pleading, of seeking to move the hand of God to change some circumstance in the world. But it is also the fast of pleading with God to change you—by bringing your heart in line with his highest purpose and opening your eyes to the deeper revelation of himself that he is longing for you to see.

MAKE IT REAL!

What deep issue or struggle have you been wrestling with God over in recent months? Name it, and then invite a few of your friends to join you in a multi-day fast to seek God regarding that issue or question. As much as possible, keep your schedule clear of distractions during the fast so you can focus your full attention on prayer. After the fast, gather your friends together and discuss your experience. What did you discover? How did God reveal himself? What did he say?

THE FAST OF RESTORATION
Week 13—Wednesday

Is not this the kind of fasting I have chosen: to loose the chains of injustice and untie the cords of the yoke, to set the oppressed free and break every yoke? Is it not to share your food with the hungry and to provide the poor wanderer with shelter—when you see the naked, to clothe him, and not to turn away from your own flesh and blood? Then your light will break forth like the dawn and your healing will quickly appear then your righteousness will go before you, and the glory of the Lord will be your rear guard.
(Isaiah 58:6-8)

ONCE you have integrated the discipline of fasting into your walk with God, do not be surprised when he begins to speak to you out of the fast, calling you to be someone you did not think you were, and to do things you did not think you could do. The story of God's heart encompasses far more than any one of our lives alone, and if given the chance, he will call you to step into the larger story he is telling—to become an emissary of his power and will in the world, and a minister of his freedom and restoration to the lost and oppressed.

In the end, isn't that what our fasting and prayer have been for all along? We want God to redeem the world. We want him to rescue the oppressed, to free captive hearts and lives, to feed the hungry, to heal our diseases, to fill the empty and dark places of the world with his unquenchable hope and light.

Perhaps what the discipline of fasting ultimately teaches us all is not merely that God shares our desire to redeem the world…but that he has chosen to redeem the world through us.

MAKE IT REAL!

Several Christian organizations and denominations sponsor nationwide fasts at various times of the year to seek God regarding some of the major issues facing the world. Ask your church leader how to find more information about these nationwide fasts. Once you have researched them, make a commitment to participate in one or more in the coming year.

Then Jesus came to them and said, "All authority in heaven and on earth has been given to me. Therefore go and make disciples of all nations, baptizing them in the name of the Father and of the Son and of the Holy Spirit, and teaching them to obey everything I have commanded you. And surely I am with you always, to the very end of the age."
(Matthew 28:18-20)

EVANGELISM as a practice has fallen into disfavor among many Christians in recent decades. A few televangelists, driven by greed and the lust for fame, have made a mockery of the holy practice of sharing faith and cast a long shadow of suspicion across the church as a whole. Thankfully, whenever these charlatans appear, they usually quickly become the laughing stock of the culture at large, who see through the veneer of their on-screen performance more easily than most believers.

In fact, perhaps it is the church and not those outside it who are most confused by this controversial debacle. We ask ourselves, "Is this really what evangelism is about—a bunch of yelling and sweating and the waving of arms, all carefully designed to whip a crowd into a frenzy so they will come forward, make a decision, and fill out a card?" In our hearts, we know it is not.

But then what is evangelism supposed to be?

The Great Commission is often bandied about as the urgent impetus for pressuring those outside the church to "make a decision for Christ." But Jesus never commands us to make converts. He commands us to make *disciples*—and that is a very different objective indeed. The goal of sharing faith is not conversion, but whole life transformation. To make a disciple for Jesus does not require high pressure sales techniques or fevered pleas to sign on the dotted line. All it requires is heart of compassion, humble dependence on the power of God, and a willingness to engage in an ongoing relationship with a lost and hurting world.

MAKE IT REAL!

When you hear the word *evangelist,* what image comes to mind? In your journal, write a description of the quintessential "evangelist." Is it a man or a woman? What's he wearing? How does she talk? What sorts of things does he typically say? When you're finished, read through your description. What do you notice? If you were to write a description of what an evangelist looks like based solely on scripture, how would it be different?

THE MESSAGE OF YOUR LIFE

But in your hearts set apart Christ as Lord. Always be prepared to give an answer to everyone who asks you to give the reason for the hope that you have. But do this with gentleness and respect.
(1 Peter 3:15)

I often hear Christians jokingly complain that they would gladly share their faith more often if only someone would actually ask them to "give the reason for the hope" within them. When I hear this complaint, I immediately think one of two things must be true about the complainer: Either he has no close, ongoing relationships with nonChristians or else his life fails to demonstrate any hope worth asking about. Neither alternative is acceptable.

In Matthew 5:16, Jesus commanded us to "let your light shine before men, that they may see your good deeds and praise your Father in heaven." What is the nature of the light you are shining out into the world? What is the light shining on most of the time? What does this light of yours inspire others to do?

Let me frame it another way. Think for a moment about the message your life is broadcasting to the world. In other words, if someone filmed a documentary of your life and then broadcast it to the world, what's the primary message your documentary would convey about life? about God? about the gospel? Imagine if the documentary had no sound—like a silent movie—what would the message be then? What if it were only sound with no picture—what message is getting broadcast there?

The point is this: As followers of Christ, we are called to inspire hope in the world. The message of our lives—in word, in action, in every way possible—should be nothing less than the gospel itself. Remember, the gospel is a *good message!* But you cannot share it powerfully unless it is first powerfully living in you.

MAKE IT REAL!

If you had to narrow your life's message down to a single statement, what would it be? Write it down, then ask two of your closest friends what they see as the primary message of your life. Discuss together what Jesus wants the primary message of your lives to be. If your life really were broadcasting that message, what would it look like? Pray together, asking God to refine your life to reflect the message he wants to share through you.

TAKE a few moments this weekend to review the devotions you've read over this past week, as well as the "Make It Real!" steps you've done. As you reflect on the week, get curious about how God is moving in and through your life. Use these questions as a guide:

❖ What insights have you gained over the past week?
❖ What changes or shifts are you noticing in your relationship with God? with others? with yourself?
❖ What "Make It Real!" steps were the most meaningful for you? What made them meaningful?
❖ How will you live differently next week as a result of what you've learned?
❖ What support do you need to help you make that change?
❖ Based on your experiences over the past week, what do you most need from God right now?
❖ What do you suppose God might be wanting most from you right now?

CHALLENGE: If you missed one of the "Make It Real!" steps for this week, set aside time this weekend to complete it, and record your reactions, insights, and results in your journal.

THE POWER TO SHARE
Week 14—Monday

But you will receive power when the Holy Spirit comes on you;
and you will be my witnesses in Jerusalem, and in all Judea and
Samaria, and to the ends of the earth.
(Acts 1:8)

THE disciples had witnessed many wonders in their time with
Jesus. They'd seen the lame rise up and walk, the blind see, the
dead raised back to life, and a few loaves and fish multiplied to
feed thousands. These men and women had actually witnessed
these miracles with their own eyes! What's more, they had
listened firsthand to Jesus' message of salvation over and over
again. They were fully convinced. They knew he was the
Messiah, the Christ, the Son of God. If anyone was qualified to
testify to the world about who Jesus was, they were. And so it is
vital that we notice that Jesus commanded them not to say a
word—not even to go out in public—until they had first received
power from on high.

Being a witness for Jesus isn't about cleverness, or
knowledge, or the colorfulness of your experiences with God. It's
about power—that is, the revelation of God's power in and
through you. As the Apostle Paul explained to the Corinthians, "I
came to you in weakness and fear, and with much trembling. My
message and my preaching were not with wise and persuasive
words, but with a demonstration of the Spirit's power, so that
your faith might not rest on men's wisdom, but on God's power"
(1 Corinthians 2:3-5).

As followers of Christ, we are all sealed with the gift of the
Holy Spirit. But that does not automatically mean we are filled
with the Spirit's power. On the contrary, we are commanded to
"be filled with the Spirit" (Ephesians 5:18) so that the anointing
of his power on our lives may be continually evident to all.

How is the Spirit's power being revealed through you these
days? Let your voice speak from there, boldly and without
apology. And watch God's power work through you to change
lives.

MAKE IT REAL!

When was the last time you shared what God was doing in your life with a nonChristian? This week, ask God to provide an opportunity to do just that. Don't make it about trying to convert anyone. Just share your story, friend to friend, and invite God to reveal himself through you. Notice what happens—not just in the other person, but in you.

YOUR CALL TO DISCIPLE
Week 14—Tuesday

And the things you have heard me say in the presence
of many witnesses entrust to reliable men
who will also be qualified to teach others.
(2 Timothy 2:2)

GOD has commissioned us all as shapers of lives. Because of his Spirit within us, we influence the hearts of all those who cross our path. We shine the light of Jesus wherever we go, whatever we do. As Paul once observed, it is as though Christ is entreating the world through us (2 Corinthians 5:20). He is, in fact, within us—in our eyes, in our touch, in the tenor of our voices—wooing, welcoming, guiding, touching. Beckoning a world of souls to come, be healed, and follow him.

"…do you not recognize this about yourselves," writes Paul, "that Jesus Christ is in you…?" (2 Corinthians 13:5, NASB). Because of the incarnation of Christ within us, the Christian journey is inherently relational. It is not a philosophy or a denomination or a political party that we follow, but a Person. He is alive within us, and the journey we take with him is one of becoming.

It follows, then, that sharing him with others would be equally relational. In fact, the forging of a strong relationship is essential to disciple making. If you doubt it, look to the way Jesus mentored his own disciples! Inspiring others to become passionate followers of Christ is as much about sharing your life as it is about sharing your theology. In fact, if you never bare your heart to those you wish to influence, then all your rich theology won't mean much anyway.

By the very nature of our salvation, we carry Christ with us wherever we go. To share him…to persuade others to follow him…all that is required is a conscious surrender to his presence and power within us, and a willingness to invest our lives in those he loves.

MAKE IT REAL!

Starting this month, really step out as a Disciple Maker. Forge a mentoring relationship with at least one person over the next 12 months. In choosing your "mentee," listen closely to the leading of the Holy Spirit within you. You might work with someone in your church's high school group, or volunteer with a local outreach group, or prison ministry. Jesus will guide you to the person or persons he wants you to invest in.

A LIFESTYLE OF DEVOTION
Week 14—Wednesday

Go and shout in Jerusalem's streets. This is what the Lord says: "I remember how eager you were to please me as a young bride long ago, how you loved me and followed me even through the barren wilderness. In those days Israel was holy to the Lord, the first of my children..."
(Jeremiah 2:2-3, NLT)

A Christian recently came to a pastor friend of mine complaining about his excessive workload. "My job is so demanding," he said in frustration. "I'm working 60 hours a week now, and hardly have time for anything else."

"How is your devotion to God?" asked the pastor.

The Christian laughed sadly and shook his head. "There isn't time," he said. "I wish there were, I mean I want there to be. But I just don't have any time to devote to God right now."

"So you're telling me that you cannot fulfill your devotion to God while working 60 hours a week?"

"Yeah," the Christian replied with a shrug. "I just don't see how."

The pastor nodded. "Then I have the answer to your problem. You must stop working 60 hours a week."

The Christian laughed. But the pastor wasn't joking.

As true disciples, we know that devotion to Christ must take priority over all other commitments. It is more important than our work, more important than romance or friendship, or even our families. But what is the standard by which we measure devotion to God? Certainly, you can't gauge your level of devotion merely by what you say that it is or wish it to be. Yet neither can you measure it by the number of religious acts you commit in a given week. But if these things do not define devotion, what does? What is it to be devoted to Christ? What does a life of devotion to God really look like?

MAKE IT REAL!

Without question, Jesus epitomized a life of devotion to God. This week, read through the Gospel of Luke with the goal of discovering exactly how Jesus did it. How exactly did he live out his devotion to God? How might you apply his example to your own relationship with God?

THE ESSENCE OF DEVOTION
Week 14—Thursday

Love the Lord your God
with all your heart
and with all your soul
and with all your mind
and with all your strength.
(Mark 12:30, NIV)

IN the beginning of our Christian journey, we quickly learn to associate devotion to God with obedience to his Word. "The one who loves me will obey my Word," says Christ, and because we want to love him we set about learning what the Word has to say about the way we should live—what is right to do and wrong to think and so on. And over time we begin to set our lives in order. We discipline ourselves to study and worship and serve. We strive to think humbly and put others' needs ahead of our own. And yet, though this is all good, and we *know* it is good, it still feels somehow incomplete. We remain at our core not quite satisfied with the whole affair.

Indeed, something is missing. For obedience to the Word is only the beginning. It is vital to devotion, but it is not the ultimate goal. If it were, then Christianity would be nothing more than a religion, just like all the others. But Christianity is not a religion at all. It is a relationship.

Which of your human relationships is the deepest in terms of devotion? Think for a moment about what that devotion is like. How does it express itself? What does it create within the relationship? If you whittled your devotion down to its core essence, what would you call it?

It's love, isn't it? Simple, pure, powerful love. As Mark 12:30 describes, love lives at the heart of God's desire toward us. That is the essence of the devotion God is after in you. He wants more than your obedience. He wants you to love him.

MAKE IT REAL!

On a scale of 1 to 10, how would you rate your current level of devotion to God? If your score were one point higher, what would be different about your life? What if your score were two points higher—what would your life look like then? In your journal, create a list of possible changes you could make in your life to raise your score all the way to 10. Then choose one to try out this week.

THE ACTS OF DEVOTIONS
Week 14—Friday

But I am afraid that just as Eve was deceived by the serpent's cunning, your minds may somehow be led astray from your sincere and pure devotion to Christ.
(2 Corinthians 11:3)

AT its core, devotion is simply love for God demonstrated and proven over time. For that reason, devotion to God is not a quality we come by quickly. You don't get there by making one grand decision, but rather by making a thousand little decisions, over a period of many years, each one a simple demonstration of your ongoing commitment to love him well. But what are these small choices? On a practical level, what does a life of devotion to God actually look like?

Again, it is helpful here to consider what devotion looks like on the human level to better understand how it ought to look with God. When you are devoted to someone—say, your spouse, for example—what sorts of things do you naturally do to demonstrate that devotion and keep it alive? What do you do to deepen it? Begin by looking there, and you will soon find many ideas for deepening your devotion to God as well.

Of course, our devotion to God goes beyond that which we offer friends or family. When you are devoted to God, your relationship with him becomes your preeminent concern. All of your decisions—from how many hours you work to what you eat or drink to what you choose to do for fun—all revolve around their impact on your communion with Christ. But perhaps the most obvious and powerful expression of devotion to God is simply the commitment to spend regular quality time with him, regardless of whatever else is happening in our lives. As Brennan Manning has said, "I don't know how people say, 'I love God with all my heart and soul,' and yet don't give him any time. The people who matter in my life I make time for, not because I should or I must—I want to. The simple truth is that we move toward what we want. And when you find a desire that transcends all the other desires, it really grips your life."

MAKE IT REAL!

Where is God's Spirit leading you to share his mercy with the world? Spend some time this week online investigating various opportunities available for giving and serving others in the name of Christ. You can begin your search at www.charitynavigator.org, a site devoted to monitoring thousands of giving and service organizations. Ask God to lead you to one or more opportunities to pursue this month.

WEEKEND REFLECTION

TAKE a few moments this weekend to review the devotions you've read over this past week, as well as the "Make It Real!" steps you've done. As you reflect on the week, get curious about how God is moving in and through your life. Use these questions as a guide:

- ❖ What insights have you gained over the past week?
- ❖ What changes or shifts are you noticing in your relationship with God? with others? with yourself?
- ❖ What "Make It Real!" steps were the most meaningful for you? What made them meaningful?
- ❖ How will you live differently next week as a result of what you've learned?
- ❖ What support do you need to help you make that change?
- ❖ Based on your experiences over the past week, what do you most need from God right now?
- ❖ What do you suppose God might be wanting most from you right now?

CHALLENGE: If you missed one of the "Make It Real!" steps for this week, set aside time this weekend to complete it, and record your reactions, insights, and results in your journal.

He has showed you, O man, what is good. And what does the Lord require of you? To act justly and to love mercy and to walk humbly with your God.
(Micah 6:8)

DEVOTION to God is not merely "vertical"—that is, it cannot be fully known or expressed solely in the private dimension of your life. Our devotion to him also has a horizontal dimension, extending outward to the hurting world of souls that cross your path every day.

What is the act of justice that God is wanting to accomplish through you right now? How is his Spirit prompting you to demonstrate his mercy in the world?

In a life of devotion, these are questions we must ask continually in the Spirit, and be always ready to respond with a willing heart. There is no such thing as devotion to Christ without the outward expression of his love to the world. As John wrote, "Whoever does not love does not know God, because God is love" (1 John 4:8). Indeed, it is our willingness to love the world, even at great personal cost, that most clearly identifies us as belonging to God. The simple truth is that God is out there in the world right now—comforting the orphan with AIDS in South Africa, extending hope to the shattered heart of the Nepalese girl sold into the sex trade, holding the hand of the mother in Sudan whose children have no place to lay their heads tonight. And if we are devoted to him in love, we will follow him there, too.

MAKE IT REAL!

Commit an entire month to deepening your devotion to Jesus. Invite a few friends to join you in studying together one of the books in the "Book Recommendations" list. Read through a few chapters every week, then discuss the book together and share how its message can help you deepen your devotion to Christ.

BOOK RECOMMENDATIONS
The Cost of Discipleship by Dietrich Bonhoeffer
The Pursuit of God by A.W. Tozer
Desiring God by John Piper

The way of the sluggard is blocked with thorns,
but the path of the upright is a highway.
(Proverbs 15:19)

AMONG the vices that undo the work of God in a Christian's life, laziness is perhaps the least noticed or understood. Certainly it is the least feared. While we may recoil from dangerous thoughts of greed or lust or envy or pride that intrude upon our hearts, we are more apt to look upon the spirit of laziness as an irritating but largely innocuous houseguest…like the chatty neighbor next door who keeps finding ways to keep you from doing the work that most needs doing.

We have all fallen under the hazy spell of laziness at some time or another. But what exactly is this vice anyway? And what is its danger to the follower of Christ?

Laziness is known by many names. Indolence. Lethargy. Sluggishness. Idleness. Sloth. Most dictionaries define it simply as the disinclination to exert oneself. But that is really just a description of its outward effect. You have to look deeper for the truth of what indolence actually is. Only then will we understand why the Bible includes such an abundance of warnings against its dangers.

MAKE IT REAL!

Where does laziness show up in your life? Think back over the last two weeks and make a quick list of situations in which you think you gave in to laziness. When your list is complete, take a moment to look more deeply at each situation.

First of all, do a reality check. Was it really laziness? For example, perhaps you were genuinely tired, or perhaps the task at hand was not really all that important—either to God or to you.

But if it was laziness—what do you suppose caused it?

THE LAND OF INDOLENCE
Week 15—Wednesday

How long will you lie there, you sluggard? When will you get up from your sleep? A little sleep, a little slumber, a little folding of the hands to rest—and poverty will come on you like a bandit and scarcity like an armed man.
(Proverbs 6:9-11)

IMAGINE for a moment that laziness is a place—a nondescript corner in the landscape of your life. It is a dull land, void of sun, with stale, heavy air. A fog covers the ground like a blanket, shrouding whatever landmarks you might otherwise see, and making every place you stand seem pretty much like every other. Its general effect is one of dull confusion, which effectively numbs your motivation to move. You cannot tell which way you want to go. Better to stay where you are, you tell yourself, until the fog clears. But that rarely, if ever, actually happens.

For all it lacks in appeal, however, the land of laziness has a few powerfully attractive qualities: For one thing, it doesn't demand anything of you, except perhaps that you avoid meaningful thought. You can come as you are and stay as long as you like. The confusing shroud of fog, though numbing to the soul, is also quite comfortable. Overall, the land feels amazingly *safe*. Laziness, it turns out, is a wonderful place to hide.

Hide from what? Risk, perhaps. Injury. Struggle. The possibility of failure. Or even death. Whatever cost that, to you, seems unreasonable in the pursuit of God's greater call upon your life. By escaping to the land of indolence, you never have to directly refuse God's call upon your life. Then again, you never quite say yes to it either. You just effectively put off dealing with the issue until, eventually, it no longer matters.

Create a personalized description of your own "land of laziness." What kind of land is it? What colors are there? What smells do you notice? How is your land different from the one described in the devotional reading? When you're finished, share your description with a friend and discuss together how living in the land of laziness keeps you from following God with your whole heart.

THE ROOT OF LAZINESS
Week 15—Thursday

The sluggard's craving will be the death of him,
because his hands refuse to work.
(Proverbs 21:25)

THE people who live in the land of indolence, as a rule, don't quite know how they got there. Some of them, in fact, still don't seem to realize where they are. You see them standing there, quite obviously lost in a grand dream about some other place; but for all their dreaming, they are completely inert. Others brazenly deny that they are there at all, and try to prove the point by scurrying busily about, accomplishing all sorts of tasks that amount to nothing of consequence. A few others tell you they are getting ready to leave, but they never seem to go anywhere. A few even refuse to look at you, or, more importantly, at themselves.

No one wants to believe they have fallen prey to a sluggard's spirit. So to soothe our own minds, perhaps, we mask our condition with less offensive labels. We call it procrastination, avoidance, denial, daydreaming. Even excessive busyness can be a disguise for sloth—when the long list of busy tasks is simply an elaborate excuse for avoiding the real, meaningful work to which God is calling us.

Whatever its disguise, however, the spirit of indolence always has its roots in one of two sources. The first is arrogance, which fosters a laziness borne out of a sense of entitlement. Why should I have to strive and struggle for what I clearly deserve to be given? Believing themselves entitled by their own giftedness or talents, these lazy Christians impatiently wait for God to "give" them a powerful ministry, a better job, or victory over some obstacle in their lives, while stubbornly refusing to step into the pursuit of their goal in any practical way.

The second and perhaps more pervasive root of laziness, however, is fear. We fear what may happen to us if we say yes to God's great call on our lives. What if I fail? What if I look foolish? What if God doesn't come through when I need him?

And even more fear surrounds what we might be required to lose in pursuit of God's call. What if I am rejected or attacked? What if I end up poor and alone? What if I die? Rather than face such an imposing barrage of fearful questions, we opt to retreat into the cozy fog of spiritual numbness. Indolence—the dull disinclination to take action—becomes the blanket in which we hide ourselves from God's bigger vision for our lives.

MAKE IT REAL!

In your time with God this week, study the Parable of the Talents in Matthew 25:14-30, paying particular attention to the third servant in the story. Why do you suppose God judged the servant as "lazy"? What's the connection in the story between laziness and fear? What's the lesson Jesus wanted those listening to understand?

THE COST OF LAZINESS
Week 15—Friday

A sluggard does not plow in season;
so at harvest time he looks but finds nothing.
(Proverbs 20:4)

THE Bible makes it clear that the eventual price for embracing a lazy, sluggish spirit is always poverty (see Proverbs 19:15 and 24:30-34). It's easy to understand this on a natural level, of course. Any man who lies around all day and refuses to work will eventually face financial ruin. But there is also a spiritual poverty that comes out of chronic indolence—and that is far worse.

If you succumb to a lazy, shiftless spirit for long enough, your heart will begin to go numb. You will feel little—either good or bad—but in general, you will know that you are somehow less alive. You will experience an impotence of will— the apparent inability to keep your promises, especially those you make to yourself. You will find yourself remembering the person you once were as a stranger you no longer recognize. It is as if that part of your soul that is the most vibrant and alive has fallen asleep. And in the dull comfort of your dream you have forgotten all about the true potential of your life with God in the waking world.

Thankfully, the Bible also identifies the antidote for an indolent heart. "The sluggard craves and gets nothing," says Proverbs 13:4, "but the desires of the diligent are fully satisfied." Diligence—the humble commitment to consistent, daily obedience to God's purpose planted in your heart—marks the path that leads out of the land of indolence and back to the rich heartland of courage and faith. Do not settle for a comfortable, numb, unremarkable life. You were made for something far greater than ordinary. Wake up your heart, summon your courage, and commit yourself to action today.

MAKE IT REAL!

Commit yourself to developing a diligent attitude of obedience to God's call. Invite a few friends to join you in studying together one of the books in the "Book Recommendations" list. Read through a few chapters every week, then discuss the book together and share how its message can help you avoid a spirit of laziness and pursue God's will with a heart of passion.

BOOK RECOMMENDATIONS
The Purpose Driven Life by Rick Warren.
The Dream Giver by Bruce Wilkinson
Living Above the Level of Mediocrity by Charles Swindoll

WEEKEND REFLECTION

TAKE a few moments this weekend to review the devotions you've read over this past week, as well as the "Make It Real!" steps you've done. As you reflect on the week, get curious about how God is moving in and through your life. Use these questions as a guide:

- ❖ What insights have you gained over the past week?
- ❖ What changes or shifts are you noticing in your relationship with God? with others? with yourself?
- ❖ What "Make It Real!" steps were the most meaningful for you? What made them meaningful?
- ❖ How will you live differently next week as a result of what you've learned?
- ❖ What support do you need to help you make that change?
- ❖ Based on your experiences over the past week, what do you most need from God right now?
- ❖ What do you suppose God might be wanting most from you right now?

CHALLENGE: If you missed one of the "Make It Real!" steps for this week, set aside time this weekend to complete it, and record your reactions, insights, and results in your journal.

The Lord Almighty is the one you are to regard as holy, he is the one you are to fear, he is the one you are to dread, and he will be a sanctuary; but for both houses of Israel he will be a stone that causes men to stumble and a rock that makes them fall. And for the people of Jerusalem he will be a trap and a snare.
(Isaiah 8:13-14)

EARLY in my Christian journey, I was fortunate enough to be discipled by a great woman of God by the name of June. She spent many sleepless nights praying for my spiritual growth, as well as the spiritual growth of several of my friends. On many occasions she taught us from the Word, and always provided an example of godliness that I will never forget.

Anytime one of us asked her what it was really like to follow Christ for as many years as she had, she would grin mischievously, wiggle her finger in our faces, and say, "If you can be offended, you will be offended." She would never explain what she meant. And for years I never understood it. But then God did something in my life that I considered to be deeply unfair, and I withdrew from him for a few difficult years. Eventually I repented of my pride, and once again gave to him my full heart. On the day I did that, June's words suddenly echoed back into my thoughts. *If you can be offended, you will be offended.*

And then I understood. Pride is the enemy of the grace of God. And those who choose to walk with Jesus should expect that he will consistently and repeatedly confront them at the point of their pride, so as to shatter it. He will do the very thing that your pride says he must not do. He will offend you. He doesn't do this to push you away, but rather to set you free. For Jesus recognizes what we in our pride fail to see: that our arrogance is a prison, and until the walls of arrogance are broken down around our hearts, we will never be free.

MAKE IT REAL!

When was the last time God did something (or failed to do something) that deeply offended you? In your journal, write a quick synopsis of what happened. Afterward, write a synopsis again, but this time, describe what happened from God's point of view. What do you suppose God was trying to accomplish in you? What point of pride might he have been pressing against?

What causes fights and quarrels among you? Don't they come from your desires that battle within you? You want something but don't get it. You kill and covet, but you cannot have what you want. You quarrel and fight... You adulterous people, don't you know that friendship with the world is hatred toward God? Anyone who chooses to be a friend of the world becomes an enemy of God. Or do you think Scripture says without reason that the spirit he caused to live in us envies intensely? But he gives us more grace. That is why Scripture says: "God opposes the proud but gives grace to the humble."
(James 4:1-6)

IT is the nature of pride to blind us to its presence within us. We can usually think of several people we know who are prideful, but we rarely consider ourselves to be like them. Sure, we may struggle with a prideful attitude or thought now and again, but it's nothing compared to the arrogance of those other people. They've really got a problem with it. We don't. Right?

When we first come to God we are, every one of us, saturated with pride. And chances are very good that we will still be carrying around a significant load of pride for many years into our journey with God. It's important to understand this because one of the first things pride does to maintain its hold within us is to try and convince us it isn't there. Pride is a sneaky vice—as easy to spot in others as it is difficult to see in ourselves. But there are ways to recognize it, if you are willing to look.

"Pride goes before destruction, a haughty spirit before a fall" (Proverbs 16:18). The word *destruction* in this proverb literally means a "fracture" or a "breaking." It implies ruining something by breaking or injuring it in some way. Pride always leaves a trail of strife, injury, and fractured relationships in its wake. Does relationship with you involve a lot of emotional drama and strife? Are you easily offended by others' actions or words? Are you quick to strike back (openly or in a passive aggressive way) at those who upset you? Do you harbor grudges, or find it easy to pass judgment on other people's motives? Do you cause or contribute to division within your church, work, or social circles? If you answer yes to any of these, then you can be sure that your soul is in the grip of pride.

MAKE IT REAL!

Sit down with two or three of your closest friends and ask them to honestly respond to these questions: Does relationship with me typically involve a lot of emotional drama and strife? Am I easily offended by your actions or words? Am I quick to strike back at you when I'm upset? Do you think I find it easy to pass judgment on other people's motives? Listen humbly to their responses, and then ask them to pray with you for God to open your eyes to any pride in your heart.

But if you harbor bitter envy and selfish ambition in your hearts,
do not boast about it or deny the truth. Such "wisdom" does not
come down from heaven but is earthly, unspiritual, of the devil.
For where you have envy and selfish ambition, there you find
disorder and every evil practice.
(James 3:14-16)

OUR culture applauds ambition. Whether in the realm of
business, entertainment, or politics, those who conquer the
competition and rise to the top of the societal heap—especially
against the odds—are praised and admired as stunning examples
of success. We love to talk about them in the break room, or
listen to them being interviewed on television, or read the books
they write about their fight to the top. We tend to think of them as
wise, and we want to learn their secrets. Often, we envy them.

But before we envy them too much, it would be wise to take a
second look. Who is the champion of their story? For whose
glory and fame are they working so hard?

Selfish ambition is the obstinate desire to gain personal
recognition, power or success for your own glory. It is one of the
worst manifestations of pride, because it not only cuts you off
from God's greater purpose for your life, but also—as James
points out—corrupts your heart with disorder and a willingness to
compromise with evil ways. It doesn't take long for a person
trapped in the snare of selfish ambition to have a difficult time
perceiving any error in his attitude at all. "What's wrong with
wanting to be successful?" he might argue. "I've worked hard to
get where I am, and I deserve to reap the rewards of my efforts."

But God's response to such arrogance is stern. "You fool!
This very night your life will be demanded from you. Then who
will get what you have prepared for yourself?" (Luke 12:20).

There is an ambition that God applauds. It is the ambition to
spread God's fame, to love him well, and to fully accomplish his
purpose for your life. But selfish ambition—seeking success or

fame for the sake of your own glory or comfort—is the antithesis of loving God and will never lead you to true success.

THE RELUCTANT HEART
Week 16—Thursday

A man who remains stiff-necked after many rebukes
will suddenly be destroyed—without remedy.
(Proverbs 29:1)

WHEN we first come to God, we are very much like diamonds
in the rough—and he, the Master diamond cutter. He sees within
our rough hewn edges the multi-faceted gem we were meant to
be, and with his expert tools begins to cut away the imperfections
to reveal the diamond within. But when our hearts are deceived
by pride, our souls become hard and resistant to his blade. We
fight against the cuts he is trying to make. In response, he
increases the pressure. But pride provokes us to dig in our heels.
Eventually, if we resist the pressure of his Spirit long enough,
something in the diamond of our souls will crack. The part of you
the Holy Spirit was trying to shape is ruined, and he must now
cut it away. The glory you could have had is now diminished.
You are still a diamond in his hands—but a smaller one than
before.

That is something of the process described in Proverbs 29:1.
Pride makes us defiant toward God, resistant to his shaping
presence in our lives. If we resist long enough, something of his
great plan for our lives will be lost. We are still his, but we will
never be all that he wanted for us to become.

When God presses against a troubled area of your life, how
do you typically respond? Is your heart willing and submissive to
God's hand? In what area of your life does your heart resist him,
or even refuse him? Make a habit of noticing your reactions to
God's work in your life. And where you see the evidence of
pride, be quick to repent and submit to his leading. Doing this
will insure that you will lose none of the blessings he has
prepared for you in this life and the next.

MAKE IT REAL!

Sometime this week, set aside a day to fast before God. Focus the time on consciously humbling yourself before God and inviting his Spirit to search your heart and reveal any prideful ways in you. Keep a journal of your experience that includes specific ideas for maintaining an attitude of humility toward God once the fast is over.

See to it that no one misses the grace of God and that no bitter root grows up to cause trouble and defile many.
(Hebrews 12:15)

THE work of God is hindered most not by the outspoken enemies of the cross; but rather, by those who claim to love and follow Christ, yet miss his grace and fall into a state of bitterness.

What does it mean to miss the grace of God? How will you know if you are falling short of it? Earlier in the book, the writer of Hebrews provides a picture of what it looks like to miss God's grace: "Land that drinks in the rain often falling on it and that produces a crop useful to those for whom it is farmed receives the blessing of God. But land that produces thorns and thistles is worthless and is in danger of being cursed. It the end it will be burned" (Hebrews 6:7-8). Jesus pointed to this same condition when he said, "If anyone does not remain in me, he is like a branch that is thrown away and withers; such branches are picked up, thrown into the fire and burned" (John 15:6).

You can know whether the grace of God is at work and increasing in your life by giving an honest and thorough answer to this simple question: What is your life producing?

I am not referring to your net worth, or to the projects and tasks you complete each week through your career, though those are not without merit. Rather, this question goes deeper, to the heart—specifically, to *your* heart. What sort of *life* is your heart producing? What is the impact of that life on those around you?

God pours grace on many who do not take it to heart. They crave God's grace, but hold it at a distance, like a holy grail from which they are not worthy to drink. Or else they stubbornly refuse to embrace their helplessness and instead strive to "do" the Christian life on their own. They claim to have the Answer, but never actually possess the Life it promises. They are fields of thorns and thistles; they are branches severed from the Vine. In such a state, their hearts inevitably grow bitter, and defile those around them, even as they claim to be living in the truth.

"By their fruit you will recognize them. Do people pick grapes from thornbushes, or figs from thistles?" (Matthew 7:16). Beware of those who name Christ as Lord but whose lives consistently produce strife, judgment and bitterness in those around them.

And watch yourself.

MAKE IT REAL!

Time for a moment of honesty. In your journal, write your responses to these questions: What is your life producing? If your life were an orchard, what sort of fruit is that orchard producing? What is the general impact of that fruit on those around you?

TAKE a few moments this weekend to review the devotions you've read over this past week, as well as the "Make It Real!" steps you've done. As you reflect on the week, get curious about how God is moving in and through your life. Use these questions as a guide:

- ❖ What insights have you gained over the past week?
- ❖ What changes or shifts are you noticing in your relationship with God? with others? with yourself?
- ❖ What "Make It Real!" steps were the most meaningful for you? What made them meaningful?
- ❖ How will you live differently next week as a result of what you've learned?
- ❖ What support do you need to help you make that change?
- ❖ Based on your experiences over the past week, what do you most need from God right now?
- ❖ What do you suppose God might be wanting most from you right now?

CHALLENGE: If you missed one of the "Make It Real!" steps for this week, set aside time this weekend to complete it, and record your reactions, insights, and results in your journal.

BECOMING "ONE"
Week 17—Monday

*If you have any encouragement from being united with Christ, if
any comfort from his love, if any fellowship with the Spirit, if any
tenderness and compassion, then make my joy complete by being
like-minded, having the same love, being one in spirit and
purpose. Do nothing out of selfish ambition or vain conceit, but
in humility consider others better than yourselves. Each of you
should look not only to your own interests, but also to interests of
others. Your attitude should be the same as that of Christ Jesus.*
(Philippians 2:1-5)

WHAT is it to be "like-minded" with the other Christians in
your church or small group? Does it mean you must agree with
them on every point of theology or methodology or political
thought? No (thankfully!). Rather, the Greek word translated
"like-minded" means to share the same intention, sentiment, or
disposition. In other words, it means that we humbly recognize
that all true Christians share the same foundational desire—to
know, love, and follow Jesus—and that each of us is doing his or
her best to attain that goal. A unified family is not one that agrees
on every issue or behavior. Rather, its unity comes from its
unwavering devotion to one another's hearts. A healthy, loving
family will keep believing in you and loving you even when it
doesn't agree with your politics or your lifestyle choices. So it is
with the Body of Christ.

Who is the Christian in your church or small group that you
are most prone to judge? What makes you want to judge them?
Imagine for a moment that God has brought that person into your
life as his instrument to teach you something vitally important
about his desire for oneness in the Body. What do you suppose
that lesson might be?

And what about those believers who live beyond the walls of
your particular flavor of Christianity? There are Christians who
consider themselves Mainline, Evangelical, Catholic,
Charismatic, Greek Orthodox, Independent, or something
different. What is your attitude toward those in Christ's Body

who are not like you, or do not practice their faith the way you think they should? Here is a challenge: What if you began to consider *those* Christians as more important than yourself (as scripture instructs)? What would happen? Look there and you will begin to understand the sort of oneness and unity God is after in you.

MAKE IT REAL!

In your journal, list the people in your church or extended church family whom you've felt tempted to judge for their attitude, beliefs, or behaviors. Next to each person's name, list one or more possible lessons about unity God may be trying to teach you through that person.

THE SPIRIT OF DIVISION
Week 17—Tuesday

Get rid of all bitterness, rage and anger,
brawling and slander, along with every form of malice.
Be kind and compassionate to one another, forgiving each other,
just as in Christ God forgave you.
(Ephesians 4:31-32)

A divisive spirit is one that is prone to pass judgment on the heart of another Christ follower. We are all capable of falling in league with this spirit, though we are often slow to recognize it because it usually comes upon us when we have in some way been wronged by another's actions. Someone in your small group snaps at you, so you label their heart as insensitive or immature. Your prayer partner betrays a confidence, so you slander her in return. Your pastor does something to offend you, and you complain about him behind his back. Before you know it, you have become an accomplice to the enemy of God.

The best way to recognize a divisive spirit within yourself or others is to watch for its fruits: A critical or dismissive attitude, slander, gossip, and a subtle willingness to perceive others according to some "label" instead of as whole human beings. Such arrogance lies at the root of all unhealthy division within the church. The simple fact is that casting judgment on another person's heart is off limits for Christians. We simply don't have the necessary purity, wisdom or spiritual authority to judge any other human being. Like the Pharisees in Jesus' day, we are in no position to throw stones.

I am not saying, of course, that we should never judge another person's behavior. What a person *does* is an entirely separate issue from who a person *is*. We have all been used as an instrument of evil at one time or another in our lives. But that does not mean that "evil" defines who we are. Rather, who we are is defined by God. And for those who have placed their faith in Jesus, that definition is clear and beyond reproach.

Beware of condemning in your arrogance the heart that God has approved.

MAKE IT REAL!

Ask your most trusted Christian confidant to reflect back to you what he or she sees in your behavior when it comes to gossip, slander, or any divisive attitude regarding other Christians. Listen humbly, and pray thoroughly over what you discover.

Therefore, as God's chosen people, holy and dearly loved, clothe yourselves with compassion, kindness, humility, gentleness and patience. Bear with each other and forgive whatever grievances you may have against one another. Forgive as the Lord forgave you. And over all these virtues put on love, which binds them all together in perfect unity.
(Colossians 3:12-14)

COMPASSION is the antidote for a divisive spirit, and that is where you must look to find your way past the temptation to judge those who offend your heart. You must have compassion for the heart of the one who attacks you, or disagrees with you, or offends you by their choices. It is not always an easy path. But it is the only way to truly experience victory over the struggle.

It's no wonder that Jesus commanded us to pray for our enemies, for he foresaw that many times our worst "enemies" in this world would turn out to be our brothers and sisters in the Lord. The church has always wounded its own more harshly and deeply than any pagan group outside its walls. And when you are speared or struck down, it's all too easy to vilify your attacker by saying, "He couldn't possibly be a member of God's family!" But that is a judgment you cannot afford to make.

Instead, admit your pain. Let yourself feel every bit of what you are feeling. Then ask, "What does love demand of me? What would love have me do in response to this?" As Paul indicated, love is the binding force behind the unity of Christ's body. By choosing love, you choose mercy, compassion, patience, humility, and all the other virtues that lead to unity and peace within the Body.

And besides, to follow love's path is always the correct choice, whether your enemy is a Christian or not.

MAKE IT REAL!

Who among your Christian brothers and sisters has most deeply injured your soul? Write their names in your journal. Next to each name, write your answer to the question, "What does love want of me in this situation? What would love have me do in response to this person?" Then, sometime in the next four weeks, do it.

RELIGION VS. A HEART SET FREE
Week 17—Thursday

Woe to you, teachers of the law and Pharisees, you hypocrites!
You travel over land and sea to win a single convert,
and when he becomes one, you make him twice as much
a son of hell as you are.
(Matthew 23:15)

THE Pharisees arose in the culture of Israel some 150 years before the time of Christ. Their name means "separated ones," and their emergence sprang out of a desire to bring God's people back to a pure devotion to God's law and his ways. They were revolutionaries in the respect that they believed the holy laws that governed activities within the temple should be applied just as fervently by all people within the context of their everyday lives. They meant to extend the practice of "holy living" beyond the realm of the priestly order and usher in a new age of holiness and purity among all the people of God.

It's important that we know this about their history so that we will not be too quick to distance ourselves from them, or consider their ways and desires to be so foreign to our own in the matters of God and faith. Jesus called them "sons of hell" not because they were passionate for God's purity and holiness, but because somewhere along the path their desire for good got co-opted by their own subtle arrogance, poisoning what could have been a powerfully redemptive movement and twisting it into a judgmental and controlling religion that served not God, but Satan.

The same subtle arrogance that blinded the Pharisees still lives today. It is alive in every church, in every corner of the globe. It is perhaps the greatest threat to the life of every Christian, and to the global redemptive mission Jesus came to earth to achieve. There is a reason that the bulk of Jesus' criticism and wrath was reserved for the Pharisees—not because of the men themselves, but because of the evil spirit behind the men that blinded them from the very truth they claimed to understand.

MAKE IT REAL!

Invite your friends or small group to study the history of the Pharisees. Work together to create a clear timeline of the Pharisees' history, and explore what caused their movement to degrade into the religious travesty they became. What lessons from their story can you apply to your own walk with God?

THE SEEDS OF RELIGIOUS BONDAGE
Week 17—Friday

We do not dare to classify or compare ourselves with some who commend themselves. When they measure themselves by themselves and compare themselves with themselves, they are not wise.
(2 Corinthians 10:12)

PHARISEEISM—or what I prefer to simply call religious bondage—is a danger for all followers of Christ in part because it springs from the seemingly innocent desire to be right. We want to be assured that we are living in the right way, doing the right things, and generally behaving in ways that God would approve. So we set up boundaries around our lives. We set up rules. We set up principles and disciplines and practices. In doing these things (all of which are fine and good in and of themselves), we fail to notice that we are skirting the edge of a dangerous precipice. If we are not mindful of the danger, we are very likely to slip into deception. We will begin to divide the world in terms of "us" and "them," and quietly believe that being "us" is somehow intrinsically better or more righteous than a whole assortment of "them's" that cross our path. And the worst part is that we will not even realize that we have fallen over the edge.

The desire to be right is often nothing more than a smoke screen for subtler desires that pull us toward deception. For example, the desire to earn God's approval, so you feel more deserving of his love. The desire to reduce your relationship with God to a series of formulas, so you feel more in control and pretend you are not afraid. The desire to compare yourself with others, or to establish yourself as "right" and others as "wrong," so that you will feel safe and justified in your choices. All of these are the seeds of religious bondage. Left unchecked, they will all lead you to experience the same blindness the Pharisees suffered, and unwittingly cause you to impose that same bondage on others—all in the name of righteousness.

Not God's righteousness, of course, but your own.

MAKE IT REAL!

Ask three of your nonChristian friends to tell you how your faith has impacted them, for good or bad. Listen for any sign that they experience you as hypocritical or judgmental. If they do, take heed. (And if you don't have three nonChristian friends, then get some!)

WEEKEND REFLECTION

TAKE a few moments this weekend to review the devotions you've read over this past week, as well as the "Make It Real!" steps you've done. As you reflect on the week, get curious about how God is moving in and through your life. Use these questions as a guide:

- ❖ What insights have you gained over the past week?
- ❖ What changes or shifts are you noticing in your relationship with God? with others? with yourself?
- ❖ What "Make It Real!" steps were the most meaningful for you? What made them meaningful?
- ❖ How will you live differently next week as a result of what you've learned?
- ❖ What support do you need to help you make that change?
- ❖ Based on your experiences over the past week, what do you most need from God right now?
- ❖ What do you suppose God might be wanting most from you right now?

CHALLENGE: If you missed one of the "Make It Real!" steps for this week, set aside time this weekend to complete it, and record your reactions, insights, and results in your journal.

COUNTERFEIT RIGHTEOUSNESS
Week 18—Monday

*Woe to you, teachers of the law and Pharisees, you hypocrites!
You are like whitewashed tombs, which look beautiful on the
outside but on the inside are full of dead men's bones
and everything unclean. In the same way, on the outside you
appear to people as righteous but on the inside
you are full of hypocrisy and wickedness.*
(Matthew 23:27-28)

THERE is a vast gulf of difference between living so that you
will be approved by God, and living out of the knowledge that
you already are.

The latter way is based on love and grace and the assurance
of genuine faith. There is no need to keep up appearances or to
try to prove anything to other people, for you are already
approved by the only One that matters. There is also no place for
casting judgment—not on yourself, and not on anyone else. For
you have no righteousness except that which comes from Christ.
All that he has given to you has been granted as a gift—you are
no more deserving of it than any other person you encounter.
Because it is a gift, you cannot earn it, you cannot deserve it, and
you cannot claim it came from you. You are free to simply enjoy
it.

The other way—the way of the Pharisees—is based on trying
to appear righteous in order to convince God (and other people,
and yourself) that it is true. It is a burdensome way to live,
fraught with all sorts of rules and restrictions about all manner of
behaviors and habits and appearances. Such righteousness is self-
imposed, and self-created. It has nothing whatsoever to do with
the cross.

And yet, for all its obvious drawbacks, such religious
bondage is a seductive temptation for Christians. It taunts us with
the lure of praise from people, the pride of thinking we are better
than others, and the false hope that we can make God bless us
more if only we will prove to him how good we can be. At the

root of it all, however, lies the failure to believe this one simple truth: Jesus already loves you.

MAKE IT REAL!

In your journal, describe your overall experience of Christianity as a way of life. What does your Christianity bring to your life? What does it add? What's the predominant feeling it creates in your life? Do you feel more set free, or more restricted by your Christian lifestyle? Once you've written your description, ask God to show you the kind of experience of life he desires for you.

*What is more, I consider everything a loss compared to the
surpassing greatness of knowing Christ Jesus my Lord, for whose
sake I have lost all things. I consider them rubbish, that I may
gain Christ and be found in him, not having a righteousness of
my own that comes from the law, but that which is through faith
in Christ—the righteousness that comes from God and is by faith.*
(Philippians 3:8-9)

TO enjoy the gift of Christ's righteousness, you must surrender
your own. You must relinquish the belief that you are in any way
capable of rescuing yourself, or making yourself good enough, or
proving that you are not really as bad as that fellow over there. It
is a hard thing to be undeserving. It's uncomfortable. It feels
helpless. But there is no other way to receive the gift of life that
Jesus offers. Once you choose to embrace the humility of what
you are without Christ (or rather, all that you are *not* without
him), you will be free to enjoy the gift of God's righteousness,
and stop bothering over trying to manufacture your own.

How can you know if you are trapped in religious bondage?
Perhaps the best way is to notice whether or not your heart is
genuinely set free. "It was for freedom that Christ set us free;"
wrote Paul, "therefore keep standing firm and do not be subject
again to a yoke of slavery" (Galatians 5:1, NASB). Religious
bondage can make you feel safe. It can make you feel superior. It
can even make you feel comfortable and secure in your
"rightness." But it cannot set your heart free.

Only Jesus can do that.

MAKE IT REAL!

On a scale of 1 to 10 (10 being "totally set free"), how free is
your heart? After answering for yourself, ask a few of your
closest Christian friends to share how "free" they perceive your
heart to be. Then pray together for God to unleash a greater
experience of Christ's freedom in all of your lives.

After David had finished talking with Saul, Jonathan became one in spirit with David, and he loved him as himself. From that day Saul kept David with him and did not let him return to his father's house. And Jonathan made a covenant with David because he loved him as himself.
(1 Samuel 18:1-3)

DAVID was called of God to take his place as the king of Israel. He was a heart-driven man, powerful, shrewd, and willing to risk it all to stand in true faith. And yet, without Jonathan, David would have perished long before he was offered the crown. It was Jonathan's love and belief in David that shielded him from Saul in those early years, and kept his heart from sinking into the despair that often comes on those who fight alone. The knitting of their souls was an act of God, a safeguard against the Enemy's plan for David—which was, as it is for all of us, to isolate our hearts from one another, and then bleed us dry in the frail, exposed regions of our souls.

We all need a Jonathan to have any hope of achieving the call of God on our lives. In fact, we almost always need several—a full cadre of warriors surrounding our hearts, each armed and shrewd and committed to see God's call on us fulfilled. These are men and women before whom you hide no secrets, and allow no shame. Their love allows them to see you in brutal honesty as you are, but also (and more to the point) as you are destined to be in God's great call. They stand guard over the tender places of your soul. They hold faith in you when yours is weak. And they will not let you live beneath your call. They are not a luxury. You desperately need them. For without them, you simply will not become all that God has called you to be.

Who is your "Jonathan"? In your journal, list the person (or people) whom you believe God has brought to you to fill that role. Next to each name, write a description of the role they play in your pursuit of God's call on your life. Thank God for the roles they play, and commit to pray for them regularly.

What if there is no "Jonathan" in your life? If that is your situation, write a description of the kind of person you want as a Jonathan in your life, and the kind of relationship you want to have with him or her. Be detailed and specific about what you want. Then begin praying daily—with tenacity and faith—for God to bring that person into your life.

THE COMMUNAL CALL OF GOD
Week 18—Thursday

Calling the Twelve to him, he sent them out two by two
and gave them authority over evil spirits.
(Mark 6:7)

GOD'S call on our lives is always *communal* in nature. That is, it is spiritually designed to happen in the context of relationship with others. Spiritual community (that is, Body Life) forms the foundation of all that God does in and through us. Though his purpose for your life is certainly unique (no one else has a purpose or a calling exactly like yours), he never intends for you accomplish your purpose in a relational vacuum. In fact, you simply *cannot* accomplish God's will for your life apart from deep relationship with others (those of you who have tried already know this to be true). To be all that God created you to be, you need to be powerfully connected to others in the Body who know your heart and actively support your call. That is not a sign of weakness or a lack of fortitude on your part. Rather, it is the nature of the call itself.

"…he sent them out two by two and gave them authority…" We are never commissioned by God to walk alone through life. And yet, if we're honest, the opposite often feels more true. Even now, you may feel like you're standing curiously alone in the battle to follow God's will for your life. Your armor is chinked and failing, your flank is exposed, and you find yourself believing that no matter how desperately you plead for help, no one will come to stand in your defense. Perhaps you've even come to believe that your isolation must in some way be God's will, that somehow he gets glory out of watching you struggle alone.

This is not the truth. The fact that it *feels* true speaks not of God's will or his desire for your heart, but rather of Satan's desire to convince you that you are uniquely destined by God to fight alone, that you have no true allies among God's people, and that (ultimately) you are doomed to a life of spiritual isolation and loneliness.

The truth is, you cannot win this fight alone. To win the battle for your life and your calling, you must come out of hiding, risk exposing your true heart to the Family of God, ask for help, and believe.

MAKE IT REAL!

Get together with a mature Christian friend or church leader. Take a risk to be as vulnerable as you can, using these three questions to guide you: What do you think God is trying to do in your life right now? What do you see as his unique call or "vision" for your life? What do you need right now from others in the Body in order to accomplish that vision?

THERE'S POWER IN NUMBERS
Week 18—Friday

Again, I tell you that if two of you on earth agree about anything
you ask for, it will be done for you by my Father in heaven.
For where two or three come together in my name,
there am I with them.
(Matthew 18:19-20)

GOD is omnipresent, meaning that his presence is everywhere at
all times. But in Matthew 18:19-20, Jesus gives this interesting
qualifier. "Where two or three come together in my name," says
Jesus, "there am I with them." Since God is already omnipresent,
what exactly is Christ getting at here?

I believe he is speaking, once again, to the imperative of
community in the Body of Christ. Though God is everywhere
present, his presence is not everywhere *manifested*. That is, God
doesn't continually make his presence known in an experiential
way at every point in space and time. (If he did, I suspect the
whole issue of free will would become irrelevant, as we would be
so overcome by his glory that we would fall on our faces and
worship him continually.) But where two or three are gathered in
Jesus' name, "there am I." In other words, when God's people
come together in relational unity under the banner of Jesus,
God's manifested presence and power shows up.

You may know God's presence and power in the solitude of
your inner prayer chamber. But you will never know him as
powerfully or as truly as those who have learned to seek him and
serve him earnestly in the context of transparent, spiritual
community with others. We are not meant to follow Christ in
isolation, nor to fulfill his call on our lives alone. When it comes
to God's manifested presence and glory, there is definitely power
in numbers. We need each other—whether our desire is to know
God more fully, to experience his power more richly, or to fulfill
his call on our lives. For only in the context of spiritual
community is Christ's presence and power fully revealed.

MAKE IT REAL!

Where have you disconnected from transparent, authentic community with the Body of Christ? Why are you hiding? Confess your areas of struggle to your pastor or trusted Christian mentor, and ask them to help you uncover what is blocking you from stepping more intentionally into spiritual community with other Christ followers.

WEEKEND REFLECTION

TAKE a few moments this weekend to review the devotions you've read over this past week, as well as the "Make It Real!" steps you've done. As you reflect on the week, get curious about how God is moving in and through your life. Use these questions as a guide:

❖ What insights have you gained over the past week?
❖ What changes or shifts are you noticing in your relationship with God? with others? with yourself?
❖ What "Make It Real!" steps were the most meaningful for you? What made them meaningful?
❖ How will you live differently next week as a result of what you've learned?
❖ What support do you need to help you make that change?
❖ Based on your experiences over the past week, what do you most need from God right now?
❖ What do you suppose God might be wanting most from you right now?

CHALLENGE: If you missed one of the "Make It Real!" steps for this week, set aside time this weekend to complete it, and record your reactions, insights, and results in your journal.

TAKING YOUR PLACE IN THE BODY
Week 19—Monday

Just as each of us has one body with many members,
and these members do not all have the same function,
so in Christ we who are many form one body,
and each member belongs to all the others.
(Romans 12:4-5)

BRING to mind two or three of your closest Christian friends. As you project their smiling faces onto video screen of your thoughts, stop and consider this: Do you realize that, from Christ's point of view, you actually *belong* to these people? That is, as fellow members of Christ's Body, you are—at the deepest level imaginable—a part of them. And they, a part of you.

Each of you brings an essential piece of the mystery that is Christ to one another's lives. You "reveal" Christ in way no one else ever has or ever will. Each of you brings a particular manifestation of Christ's power, a particular expression of his heart, a particular revelation of his wisdom, to the others in your community of faith. Your "piece"—that is, your unique expression of Christ—is not for you alone. It is also (and, perhaps, more so) for them.

That is why you belong to them. Because without you showing up fully in relationship and bringing your gift to the others in your spiritual community, there is a unique expression of Christ they will never know.

What is your place in the Body of Christ? What is the unique role you are called to play in his community? What is the unique gift you are called to bring? It is imperative that you discover and name your unique gifting and function within the Body, and that you regularly bring that expression of Christ to those with whom you share community.

You don't just owe this to yourself or to God. You owe it to all of us. We are all members of one another—from one end of the world to the other. And when any one of us refuses to show up fully in Christ's Body, we all suffer loss.

MAKE IT REAL!

Get together with the Christian friends you thought about as you read this, and read this section together again as a group. Ask your friends to respond to the questions in this section—both for themselves and for the others in the group. Finally, ask each other, "How can we deepen our experience of Christ through our relationship with each other?" Come up with two or three ideas to explore together this month.

THE COURAGE OF DESIRE
Week 19—Tuesday

*After they prayed, the place where they were meeting was shaken.
And they were all filled with the Holy Spirit and spoke the word
of God boldly.*
(Acts 4:31)

YOU cannot successfully follow God unless you are willing to do bold things. And by "bold things," I don't just mean being a little forward or a little louder than the next guy. I mean you must be willing to take risks—big ones. You must be daring. You must make courageous choices. Some will even call your behavior brazen, or foolhardy. But that doesn't matter. You aren't following *them*.

Why is the willingness to be bold so critical to walking with God? The simple answer is, because God is a bold God. Boldness is central to his character. And if you are to follow wherever he leads, you must make peace with the whole notion of being bold as well.

Throughout the New Testament, the quality of boldness is listed as the first and most consistent evidence of being filled by the Holy Spirit. Why is it, then, that we followers of Christ are so often so timid and afraid? Could it be that we are not as filled with the Spirit of God as we think we are? Or is it more that we simply like our fear, and purposefully keep it nurtured and alive in our hearts—because it gives us a sensible, solid reason to not be reckless or wild in the Name of God?

MAKE IT REAL!

On a scale of 1 to 10 (10 being "Super Bold"), how bold would you say you are in following God? In your journal, explain why you scored yourself the way you did. Then write a description of how your life would be different if your score were three points higher.

What's stopping you from moving your walk with God to that level?

WHEN FEAR TURNS WICKED
Week 19—Wednesday

Then the man who had received the one talent came. "Master,"
he said, "I knew that you are a hard man, harvesting where you
have not sown and gathering where you have not scattered seed.
So I was afraid and went out and hid your talent in the ground.
See, here is what belongs to you."

His master replied, "You wicked, lazy servant! So you knew
that I harvest where I have not sown and gather where I have not
scattered seed? Well then, you should have put my money on
deposit with the bankers, so that when I returned I would have
received it back with interest."
(Matthew 25:24-27)

IN the Parable of the Talents, the servant who received the one talent and hid it in the ground was later judged by the master as "wicked" and "lazy." But was this assessment fair? From all indications, the servant was not intentionally trying to be wicked or lazy. Instead, he was simply *afraid*. It was his fear that prompted him to bury his talent rather than risk investing it out in the world. So, is that really wickedness? Was he really being lazy?

We all need to heed the lesson of the fearful servant. To feel fear—even terror!—at the prospect of following God's call is neither wicked nor lazy in and of itself. In fact, it's only human. But the moment you allow your fear to suppress the desire of God in your heart, the moment you shrink back from taking a risk for his Kingdom because you are afraid—then it becomes wickedness and laziness of the highest order.

Some would say that fear is the great nemesis of authentic faith. I do not think this is so. After all, to look squarely at God's great call on our lives, how could we not be afraid, at least a little? "It is a terrifying thing to fall into the hands of the living God," notes the writer of Hebrews. And though he speaks here of judgment, it is equally true of falling into his grace. So then, the great evil here is not the fear itself, but rather, the quiet choice to surrender to it.

It is impossible to follow both your fear and your faith at the same time. Like the proverbial angel and demon perched on either shoulder, both faith and fear whisper in your ear at the point of every key decision in your journey. Will you be safe, or will you be bold? Will you step out in faith or hold back in fear? No doubt you are facing a decision like that even now in some area of your life. And the sobering truth is that the path you choose in that decision will identify the sort of servant you really are.

MAKE IT REAL!

What is the "faith vs. fear" decision you are facing right now? Get together with a mature Christian friend or church leader, and tell them about it. Ask for their advice, and pray together for God to fill you with his Spirit of boldness, so you can make the choice that is most pleasing to him.

THE SPIRIT OF COURAGE
Week 19—Thursday

*For you did not receive a spirit that makes you a slave again to
fear, but you received the Spirit of sonship.
And by him we cry, "Abba, Father."*
(Romans 8:15)

IT is the Spirit of sonship that we receive in Christ, wrote the
Apostle Paul, that frees us from being slaves to fear. But how
exactly does the Spirit free us? Primarily, the Spirit of sonship
does this by filling us with the deep knowledge of belonging—
the comforting assurance that no matter what the world does to
you, no matter how it accuses or misunderstands your heart, you
are his. You are approved. You are, and always will be, his
Beloved.

But the Spirit of sonship is also a spirit of longing and desire.
We cry out, "Abba, Father," not only for joy in knowing we are
his, but also in desperation to draw him nearer. We groan for
him, wrote the Apostle Paul, as the naked longing to be clothed.
The Spirit of sonship awakens our desperate desire for the things
of God, for all that he loves in the world, for the abundant life we
gain through him. And, in turn, it is only through that awakened
desire that our true courage is born.

Think of a mother with her children. She may be a fearful
woman, literally terrified at the prospect of stepping out to serve
God in boldness. But if her children are threatened by an attacker,
she will instantly throw herself into the gap and stare down the
barrel of a gun to protect them. Why? Because her desire to keep
her children safe is stronger than her fear of being injured or
killed. No doubt, she would still be terrified. But something more
powerful than her fear has taken hold.

The Holy Spirit of sonship is like that. He supplies your heart
with courage—not by erasing your fear, but rather, by
overwhelming it with desire for God.

MAKE IT REAL!

Where is fear still holding you back from absolute surrender to God's leading in your life? List each area where fear still reigns, and begin to pray daily for God's Spirit to awaken within you a deeper desire for him in those areas of your life.

THE END OF FEAR
Week 19—Friday

*There is no fear in love. But perfect love drives out fear, because
fear has to do with punishment. The one who fears is not made
perfect in love.*
(1 John 4:18)

ONLY when your longing for God grows larger than your fear
will you begin to authentically press into your fears, and push
yourself beyond them. As you step tentatively out of your
comfort zone in pursuit of him, you will find the Spirit of
boldness there waiting to support you. You will feel a strength
you know is not your own. You will sense the flow of God's holy
power moving through you in a way you've never experienced.
This strength and power are not the result of God moving closer
to you. He is right where he has always been. Rather, it is the
result of you stepping more fully into him.

But you will also encounter something greater than strength
or power. You will find love. And it is this revelation of God's
love—more brilliant than a thousand suns, more unshakeable
than the universe itself—that will finally banish your fear.

Imagine. You will no longer be afraid.

What is it to be "perfected in love"? It is to choose to love
boldly in the Name of God and for his cause—even though you
are terrified to do it—and through that sacrificial act of devotion
and hope, uncover a love in God so vast and powerful that it
blows away all memory of fear.

MAKE IT REAL!

Get together with a few Christian friends and talk about the
things you would love to do for God if you were absolutely
fearless. Make a list of the top two or three things you would
most long to do, and ask your friends to join you in praying for
God to speak to you this month concerning his will for you in
those areas. Then, as his Spirit directs, step out of your comfort
zone and deeper into his love.

TAKE a few moments this weekend to review the devotions you've read over this past week, as well as the "Make It Real!" steps you've done. As you reflect on the week, get curious about how God is moving in and through your life. Use these questions as a guide:

- ❖ What insights have you gained over the past week?
- ❖ What changes or shifts are you noticing in your relationship with God? with others? with yourself?
- ❖ What "Make It Real!" steps were the most meaningful for you? What made them meaningful?
- ❖ How will you live differently next week as a result of what you've learned?
- ❖ What support do you need to help you make that change?
- ❖ Based on your experiences over the past week, what do you most need from God right now?
- ❖ What do you suppose God might be wanting most from you right now?

CHALLENGE: If you missed one of the "Make It Real!" steps for this week, set aside time this weekend to complete it, and record your reactions, insights, and results in your journal.

So do not throw away your confidence; it will be richly rewarded.
You need to persevere so that when you have done the will of
God, you will receive what he has promised. For in just a very
little while, "He who is coming will come and will not delay. But
my righteous one will live by faith. And if he shrinks back, I will
not be pleased with him." But we are not of those who shrink
back and are destroyed, but of those who believe and are saved.
(Hebrews 10:35-39)

TWICE in my early life, I came close to marrying. In both
situations, I secretly shopped for rings. I planned out in great
detail how I would pop the question. We talked at length about
weddings, and families, and how it all might look to go through
life hand in hand. In one case, we even went to pre-marital
counseling together. From the outside, everything looked pretty
much okay. But in each relationship, there was just one problem.
I just wasn't really all that in love.

Not that I didn't love them. I did. But as I moved toward
marriage, I just kept getting this nagging feeling deep in my spirit
that I couldn't shake. *Shouldn't I be more excited than this?* I
wondered. *Shouldn't I feel more grateful, more alive, more at*
peace, more...something? But I didn't. And when I finally got
honest with myself, I realized deep down I had always known
why. I was settling. These were great women—both of them. But
neither one was the best woman for me. And I knew it.

Thankfully, in both situations God intervened to stop us from
taking a step we'd regret. (I say "we" because the truth was, in
both cases, she was settling, too.) But I'll never forget how close
I came to throwing away my confidence in God's leading in my
life—not once but twice—all because I was afraid of going solo
or never finding love.

But, I later realized, the fear of being alone wasn't even the
real issue. For underneath that fear lurked a deeper question, one
that unsettles the heart of every Christian who's tempted to

abandon God's leading and settle for less in life: Is God really *good?* Does he *really* have my best interests at heart?

MAKE IT REAL!

Where in your life are you most tempted to compromise or "settle for less" because of fear that nothing better will come along? In your journal, write a brief description of each compromise you are being tempted to make. After the descriptions, write your response to this question: What belief are you holding about God that allows you to consider "settling" in these areas of your life?

THE BIG QUESTION
Week 20—Tuesday

He who did not spare his own Son, but gave him up for us all—
how will he not also, along with him,
graciously give us all things?
(Romans 8:32)

THE question of whether or not God is good is one that every follower of Christ must confront at some point in their journey. It does no good to try and avoid it. In fact, when the question arises in your heart, the worst thing you could do is try to shame yourself into denying it is there. "What a horrible thought. Shame on you! Of course God is good. Stop thinking such nonsense."

It's not a horrible thought. It's an honest question, and one that must be answered soundly in our spirits if we are ever to follow Christ unflinchingly with our whole heart. In fact, it is those who refuse to wrestle with the question that are in the most in danger of settling for a smaller, more mediocre life than they were created to live.

The good thing about the question "Is God good?" is that there are only two possible answers. Either he is good—and therefore does indeed have my best interests at heart in every possible way, and can therefore be completely trusted to guide me toward the life that is, without question, the absolute best and most fulfilling for my soul. Or he is not good—and therefore I should immediately stop trying to follow God at all, and apply all my energy toward building a life that seems best to me. I dare say that coming to either of these conclusions is better than staying in limbo between the two because, at least with the matter concluded, you have a clear direction to follow, while with the matter undecided, you will most certainly be confused and miserable much (if not all) of the time.

In John 10:10, Jesus proclaimed, "The thief comes only to steal and kill and destroy; I have come that they may have life, and have it to the full." Jesus' promise is clear. It is not a promise that life will always be easy or that you will always understand why he gives you this or fails to give you that. Instead, it is an assurance that God's heart is good, that he loves you, that he does indeed have your best interests at heart. And if you grasp hold of him and follow wherever he leads—no matter what—he promises that you will have life, and have it to the full.

MAKE IT REAL!

Where is fear still holding you back from absolute surrender to God's leading in your life? List each area where fear still reigns, and begin to pray daily for God's Spirit to awaken within you a deeper desire for him in those areas of your life.

TENACIOUS TRUST
Week 20—Wednesday

For this very reason, make every effort to add to your faith goodness; and to goodness, knowledge; and to knowledge, self-control; and to self-control, perseverance; and to perseverance, godliness; and to godliness, brotherly kindness; and to brotherly kindness, love. For if you possess these qualities in increasing measure, they will keep you from being ineffective and unproductive in your knowledge of our Lord Jesus Christ.
(2 Peter 1:5-8)

IT is our confidence in God's unshakeable goodness that empowers us to trust him tenaciously, especially when the circumstances and relationships in our lives do not seem to be turning out for our best. He has a higher view of things than we do. He knows our hearts better than we do. He designed each and every one of us, and is intimately aware of every hidden aspect of who we are, how we think, and what we desire. He knows—far better than we do—what will bring us life. There could be no better Person to design the life best suited for our joy and fulfillment than Christ.

Because he is good, and we trust him, we don't even need to know what lies ahead. In fact, our only responsibility on this journey is to stay connected to him, and do all we can to deepen that connection, so that we might more effectively follow his lead. We "make every effort," as the Apostle Peter admonished, to add to our faith more of *his* goodness, *his* knowledge, *his* self-control, *his* godliness…until in time we come to understand that having a rich, full, abundant life isn't found by getting married, or getting rich, or a host of other things we think we cannot live without. Rather, it is found in Christ himself. For *he* is Life.

MAKE IT REAL!

Read 2 Peter 1:5-8. Which of those "qualities of Christ" listed in the passage do you most need to add to your life right now? Choose one, and then ask a Christian friend to join you in doing a Bible study on that particular quality. Look for specific ways you and your partner can begin to build that quality into your life this month.

THE TRUE AIM OF LIFE
Week 20—Thursday

But whatever was to my profit I now consider loss for the sake of Christ. What is more, I consider everything a loss compared to the surpassing greatness of knowing Christ Jesus my Lord, for whose sake I have lost all things. I consider them rubbish, that I may gain Christ...Not that I have already obtained all this, or have already been made perfect, but I press on to take hold of that for which Christ Jesus took hold of me. Brothers, I do not consider myself yet to have taken hold of it. But one thing I do: Forgetting what is behind and straining toward what is ahead, I press on toward the goal to win the prize for which God has called me heavenward in Christ Jesus.
(Philippians 3:7-8, 12-14)

THE closer you get to Christ, the more you realize how disconnected from reality the world actually is. Most of the things that the world exalts as important or even essential to personal fulfillment—such as wealth or fame or beauty or entertainment or critical success—actually have nothing to do with fulfillment at all. The same goes for falling in love, or getting married, neither of which can guarantee to bring you fulfillment any more than jumping off a cliff guarantees you will be able to fly. It's not at all wrong to desire these things or to enjoy them if you have them. But once you draw near to Christ, you realize what folly it is to place your hope for fulfillment in any of them—even a little.

But if these things don't guarantee us the fulfillment we crave, then what will? What actually makes for a beautiful life? The Apostle Paul knew. "I consider everything a loss," he wrote, "compared to the surpassing greatness of knowing Christ Jesus my Lord." Paul knew the secret that true fulfillment, true joy, true abundance, true *Life*—is found in Christ, and no where else. To know him, to tenaciously follow his lead for your life, never settling for less than his absolute best—that is the only guaranteed way to experience the rich, abundant life your were made to live.

MAKE IT REAL!

Every day this week, make it your one ambition to stay connected to God's Spirit throughout the day, and consciously follow his lead. Set your watch to beep every hour as a reminder to sincerely invite God into your routine. As you sense him leading, follow without hesitation. At the end of the week, evaluate how the experience has impacted you. Are you more or less fulfilled than you were seven days ago? What has changed?

THE TEMPTATION TO HIDE
Week 20—Friday

*When the woman saw that the fruit of the tree was good for food
and pleasing to the eye, and also desirable for gaining wisdom,
she took some and ate it. She also gave some to her husband, who
was with her, and he ate it. Then the eyes of both of them were
opened, and they realized they were naked; so they sewed fig
leaves together and made coverings for themselves. Then the man
and his wife heard the sound of the Lord God as he was walking
in the garden in the cool of the day, and they hid from the Lord
God among the trees of the garden.*
(Genesis 3:6-8)

WHEN Adam and Eve fell from perfection, the first
consequence of their sin was an onslaught of shame. And the first
new skill that shame taught them was how to hide. They
recognized they were naked, and in their newfound shame they
sewed fig leaves to hide themselves from one another. Then God
showed up in the garden, and they hid themselves from his
presence as well.

We've been hiding from each other and from God ever since.
We hide even from ourselves. We may be haunted by the
memory of Eden, but we've learned well the lessons that sin has
taught us. Over the intervening years since that fateful day in the
garden, we've perfected the art of hiding. We hide our flaws, our
misdeeds, our fallen desires. Instead of admitting our depravity,
we focus our energy on how we appear to the external world. If
we can just find the right list of rules, the right combination of
do's and don'ts, and adhere to them with religious dedication—
surely then we will be all right. Or, at the very least, we will
appear all right.

And maybe that's the best you can hope for, you tell yourself.
But inside, if you listen, you will still hear it: That memory of
Eden won't let you go. It's crying out to be redeemed.

MAKE IT REAL!

What are all the ways that you hide yourself from others or from God? In your journal, make a list of your top five favorite ways to hide. Then ask God to give you the grace and courage to stop hiding and just be your authentic self.

WEEKEND REFLECTION

TAKE a few moments this weekend to review the devotions
you've read over this past week, as well as the "Make It Real!"
steps you've done. As you reflect on the week, get curious about
how God is moving in and through your life. Use these questions
as a guide:

- ❖ What insights have you gained over the past week?
- ❖ What changes or shifts are you noticing in your
  relationship with God? with others? with yourself?
- ❖ What "Make It Real!" steps were the most meaningful for
  you? What made them meaningful?
- ❖ How will you live differently next week as a result of
  what you've learned?
- ❖ What support do you need to help you make that change?
- ❖ Based on your experiences over the past week, what do
  you most need from God right now?
- ❖ What do you suppose God might be wanting most from
  you right now?

CHALLENGE: If you missed one of the "Make It Real!" steps
for this week, set aside time this weekend to complete it, and
record your reactions, insights, and results in your journal.

THE LURE OF IMAGE MANAGEMENT
Week 21—Monday

*Woe to you, teachers of the law and Pharisees, you hypocrites!
You clean the outside of the cup and dish, but inside they are full
of greed and self-indulgence. Blind Pharisee! First clean the
inside of the cup and dish, and then the outside also will be clean.
Woe to you, teachers of the law and Pharisees, you
hypocrites! You are like whitewashed tombs, which look beautiful
on the outside but on the inside are full of dead men's bones and
everything unclean. In the same way, on the outside you appear
to people as righteous but on the inside you are full of hypocrisy
and wickedness.*
(Matthew 23:25-28)

WE have a problem, you and I. We both want to look impressive
on the outside. We very much want others to see us as right and
good and attractive and smart and "together" and spiritually on
track. But that isn't really how life "on the inside" is for us, and
secretly we both know this. On the inside we are regularly
tripping over dead men's bones and many, many other unclean
things.

It's not that we aren't full of glory as well—we certainly are.
We bear the image of God; even in our fallen state; it is
inextricably woven into the fabric of our being. But like a
masterpiece of tapestry that has been covered in grime, we are
marred by sin and its effects. The glory that defined us before the
Fall has been obscured by the muck of sin, and we are incapable
of ridding ourselves of the stain. And so, ashamed of our fallen
condition and unable to redeem ourselves, we try to hide
ourselves instead, just as Adam and Eve did with the leaves.

And more often than not, our fig leaf of choice is legalism.

Legalism is the false belief that you can prove you are good
by keeping the rules. Legalists try to hide their fallen condition
by becoming preoccupied with how they appear to others. They
are always trying to figure out the external rules of behavior that
tell them what to wear, where to go, what to say, and how to act.
Like the Pharisees in Jesus' day, they focus all of their time and

energy on "image management." Looking good and acceptable in the eyes of others is everything to a legalist, and those who are particularly good at it grow proud of their success, and are quick to judge anyone who does not measure up to their standards.

But it's all just a masquerade. An hypocrisy of the soul. A fig leaf. Rules cannot change a person's heart; they just show where a heart needs to change. As long as you hide behind rule-keeping, you will never know the true freedom and life that Christ offers.

MAKE IT REAL!

In what ways do you focus on "image management" in your own life? This week, tell a trusted Christian friend about all the ways you try to control or "manage" the way others perceive you. Explore together what you fear might happen if you stopped trying to look acceptable in the eyes of others, and instead just let yourself be completely honest and real about where you are in your journey with God.

*Then Jesus said to the crowds and to his disciples, "The teachers
of the law and the Pharisees sit in Moses' seat. So you must obey
them and do everything they tell you. But do not do what they do,
for they do not practice what they preach. They tie up heavy
loads and put them on men's shoulders, but they themselves are
not willing to lift a finger to move them."*
(Matthew 23:1-4)

JESUS reserved some of his harshest words for the most
religious people of his day. His biggest problem with the teachers
of the law and the Pharisees was their pretense, their lack of
authenticity. These "spiritual leaders" focused their energy
exclusively on the exhaustive task of looking good in the eyes of
others. In fact, by the time Jesus' was born, the Pharisees had
come up with over 600 specific religious laws and traditions that
in their view had to be meticulously followed in order to have
God's approval. But in all of their rule-keeping, they neglected
what was most important to God's heart…that is, an inside-out
transformation of the heart and life through grace by faith.

Though Jesus never condoned wrong behavior, his life and
message focused not on external rule-keeping, but on the
incredible grace and love of God that removes from us forever
any need to pretend or hide. And so the messed up, imperfect
people of Christ's day were incredibly attracted to him because
they had already given up on pretending or hiding their
brokenness from the world. But the pretentious…the rule-
keepers…the legalists…they responded to Jesus in a wholly
different way. They wanted him dead.

The same reactions hold true today. Are you honest with the
world about your brokenness? Or are you hiding, promoting the
notion through your external behaviors that you are good? To
whatever degree each is happening, you are either drawing closer
to Jesus, or trying to snuff out his authentic presence in your life.

MAKE IT REAL!

In your journal, list the ways or areas of your life in which you feel you are genuinely drawing closer to Christ. Then list all the ways or areas where you feel you are shutting him out or pushing him away. Share your list with a trusted Christian advisor and pray together for God to show you how to begin opening your heart to him in those areas where you are currently hiding.

*"Teacher, which is the greatest commandment in the Law?"
Jesus replied: "'Love the Lord your God with all your
heart and with all your soul and with all your mind.' This is the
first and greatest commandment. And the second is like it: ' Love
your neighbor as yourself.' All the Law and the Prophets hang on
these two commandments."*
(Matthew 22:36-40)

FAR from the Pharisee's 600+ laws and traditions, Jesus
promoted only two: Love God, and Love People. And in those
two "greatest commandments" lies the antidote to legalism.
Instead of focusing on the external rules, Jesus calls us to focus
simply on loving and following God, and loving people. He does
this because he knows that genuine salvation is an inside-out
process, one that requires extreme authenticity. You simply
cannot get there by pretending.

God makes all of us unique. We're all born "originals"—
masterful works of art. But due to legalism and other religious
pressures, many of us die as "copies"—an approximation of what
someone else's external standard of behavior says we should be.
But living as a "copy" has never been God's heart for any of his
children. He alone knows who you really are. He alone knows
who he created you to be and what he created you to do. He alone
can set you free.

God's offer of grace, forgiveness, and redemption demands
that you lay down all pretense, and simply be yourself—
brokenness and all. That's the only way you can authentically
become all that God created you to be.

MAKE IT REAL!

If you're ready for life-changing challenge, try this: This month, make it your singular goal to be "totally, authentically yourself" in every circumstance and with every person in your life. Begin by writing out your own description of what it really looks like for you to be totally, authentically yourself. Then practice doing it—at home, with friends, at work, and at church.

Therefore confess your sins to each other and pray for each other
so that you may be healed. The prayer of a righteous man is
powerful and effective.
(James 5:16)

"NOBODY knew."

I don't enjoy thinking about how many times I've heard those words over the years. She struggled with an eating disorder since she was 13. Nobody knew. He drank alone five nights a week just to make the stress bearable enough to let him sleep. Nobody knew. She had an abortion at 17. Nobody knew. He dropped out of college because his porn addiction had taken over his life. Nobody knew. She believed she was too ugly for anyone to love her. He was terrified of being exposed as a fake. She was plagued by the memory of her uncle's sexual abuse. He was plagued by the memory of the abuse he'd inflicted on a girl when he was a teen.

Nobody knew.

Over the years, I've watched on the sidelines as the lives of several of my friends and acquaintances "all of a sudden" seemed to crash and burn. Revelations about their addictions, abuses, sin habits, and shattered relationships always seemed to come out of nowhere. They seemed fine on the outside, but they weren't. They were hiding—and had been for years.

As I look back on each of those sad situations, I actually don't think the addiction, or the abuse, or the sin was really what ultimately caused them to crash. I think it was the hiding. It was the self-imposed isolation. It was the irrational, shame-filled belief that "I can never tell anyone about this—ever." Shame is a soul-killer. And the only antidote—the only thing that will free you from its black infection—is unguarded confession and intentional accountability with another Christian soul.

MAKE IT REAL!

What is it about you that "nobody knows"? In your journal, write it all out—every private struggle or dark experience that you would hate for anyone to discover about you. When you're finished, read it aloud to yourself. What do you notice? What do these secrets tell you about yourself? Then read it aloud again—this time to God. And pray for him to give you the courage to share everything you've written with a trusted Christian friend.

THE STRATEGIC ALLIANCE
Week 21—Friday

Do two walk together unless they have agreed to do so?
(Amos 3:3)

ANYONE can keep their deepest struggles and dreams hidden from view if they really want to. In our weekly small groups and Bible studies and after-church dinners, we share a snippet of ourselves here and snippet there—just enough to be "real" without overburdening anybody or embarrassing ourselves. But at the end of the day, or the week, or the year, who really knows us? Who could really speak to us the truth of who we are, encourage us in the dreams that are closest to our hearts, or call us on the mat about any negative pattern in our lives? We are free agents, after all. Accountable to no one.

This is not how God intended us to live. For that reason, it's all the more important that we choose to be very intentional about seeking out people who hold us accountable and walk with us as strategic partners in our quest to follow God.

I'm not speaking merely of friendship here—though that is certainly an important aspect of all relationships within the Body of Christ. But I am talking about an intentional spiritual alliance between you and at least one other growing follower of Christ. Such a partnership is an alliance of design—meaning that you consciously create the relationship together so that it serves to keep you both on the path of growth in Christ and away from the pitfalls that have sidelined you in the past.

This is not the sort of relationship that happens by accident. You must choose it for yourself, then get out there and create it. In a way, it's like asking someone to be your running partner: You invite them to run with you on the journey toward God. They agree, and you meet to discuss what your partnership will look like. In that meeting, you lay out the guidelines of the relationship—for example, keeping things confidential and avoiding judgment or ridicule. Then you take turns laying out the facts of where you are—especially those you are loathe to tell.

You share the dreams of where you'd like to be. Then, together, you design a training plan to reach your goals.

<hr>

MAKE IT REAL!

As you think about all the people you currently know, who would you most want to have as your spiritual running partner? Write the names of your two or three top choices in your journal. Then write out a detailed description of the type of strategic spiritual partnership you would love to have with this person. What sorts of things would you want to regularly talk about? How would accountability work in your relationship? How often would you get together? How would you show support for each other? What level of confidentiality would you like the relationship to maintain?

<hr>

TAKE a few moments this weekend to review the devotions you've read over this past week, as well as the "Make It Real!" steps you've done. As you reflect on the week, get curious about how God is moving in and through your life. Use these questions as a guide:

- ❖ What insights have you gained over the past week?
- ❖ What changes or shifts are you noticing in your relationship with God? with others? with yourself?
- ❖ What "Make It Real!" steps were the most meaningful for you? What made them meaningful?
- ❖ How will you live differently next week as a result of what you've learned?
- ❖ What support do you need to help you make that change?
- ❖ Based on your experiences over the past week, what do you most need from God right now?
- ❖ What do you suppose God might be wanting most from you right now?

CHALLENGE: If you missed one of the "Make It Real!" steps for this week, set aside time this weekend to complete it, and record your reactions, insights, and results in your journal.

BLISTERING HONESTY
Week 22—Monday

Wounds from a friend can be trusted,
but an enemy multiplies kisses.
(Proverbs 27:6)

I have co-designed a strategic spiritual alliance with several different men in my life. We speak regularly, pray for one another, and actively look for ways to encourage each other toward intimacy with God and fulfilling his purpose for our lives. Our conversations have not always been easy, but they have always been life-giving.

As these relationships have deepened, I've noticed myself doing something interesting. Anytime I find myself being criticized by someone in my life—whether a stranger, an acquaintance, a family member, or a co-worker—the first thing I want to do after praying about it is take the issue to one of my spiritual partners and ask, "What do you see here? Is this person saying something valid about me or my behavior? What part of this criticism is true?"

I realize that I do this because I know that these men will be brutally honest with me about what they see or don't see in my character and my life. They will not shy away from injuring me in order to help me grow. Such blistering honesty is designed right into the relationship—and I cannot tell you how thankful I am to have it. The proverb is true: the wounds I receive from these men can be trusted because I know the motivation behind them is selfless love. Such is the power of a designed spiritual alliance, and such is the joy of knowing that there are people in your life whom you can always trust to tell you the unvarnished truth.

MAKE IT REAL!

Share this devotional entry with one or two people with whom you would like to establish a spiritual alliance. After they read it, talk together about what you would each want such a relationship to accomplish in your lives. What would you like the relationship to look like? How long would you like the relationship to last? If you are both willing, agree to try it together for a trial period of 90 days. During that "test" period, work together to iron out the kinks of the relationship, re-designing as you go any part that's not working. At the end of the 90 days, evaluate together the impact the relationship has had on your lives and decide whether you would like to continue.

THE PATH TO WISDOM
Week 22—Tuesday

He who walks with the wise grows wise,
but a companion of fools suffers harm.
(Proverbs 13:20)

NOT long after you've established strategic spiritual alliances with a few key people in your life, something unexpected will happen. You'll begin to notice the incredible power and influence of all of the *other* key relationships in your life. More specifically, you'll become keenly aware of every key relationship that drains your soul. There may be people within your inner circle of friends who do not propel you toward God or encourage you toward your life purpose. Rather, they drain and discourage you from faith and hope. They may be contentious or cynical or perpetually down or ever-suspicious of your heart. But this one thing they all share in common: They always take more from you than they give.

The net result of these relationships is *harm* to your spiritual life. Once you experience the power of purposefully "doing life" with others in a way that inspires and encourages you to grow spiritually, you'll find yourself increasingly intolerant of inner-circle relationships that pull you away from that goal. Such intolerance is neither selfish nor unloving; rather, it is wise.

"He who walks with the wise grows wise." If you establish a strategic alliance with another growing follower of Christ, you will grow in wisdom. And part of that wisdom will be the bold recognition that following Christ is as much about letting go of wrong relationships as it is about consciously building right ones.

MAKE IT REAL!

Once you establish a strategic spiritual alliance with a trusted Christ follower, prayerfully talk with them about the relationships in your inner circle. Let them ask probing questions, and reflect back to you what they see. Which of your inner-circle relationships do you need to redesign? Which ones should you consider letting go of altogether? Pray carefully, then take action.

UNFILTERED PRAYER
Week 22—Wednesday

I cry aloud with my voice to the Lord; I make supplication with my voice to the Lord. I pour out my complaint before Him; I declare my trouble before Him.
(Psalm 142:1-2, NASB)

THE first time I honestly cried out to God was in the Fall of my 17th year. It happened about 2:00 a.m., in the parking lot of Woodlawn Baptist Church, where I had been attending since I was a freshman. I knew the turf well—as well as I knew the principles of faith I had learned there. But it wasn't enough. I desperately wanted it to be enough, but it just wasn't. I needed more. I needed God himself. Not a story about God; not a theory about God; not a suspicion about God's nature or a quaint teaching on his ways in the world. I needed God, the real deal…*him*. I genuinely needed to know whether God was real, and if he was real, whether he was good and worth trusting.

So I cussed him out. I dared him to show himself. I actually dared him to kill me—right there, on the spot. It was, admittedly, an emotionally desperate and immature move. But I figured that if I couldn't entice him to reveal himself by my good behavior, then I would provoke him out of the shadows through my brazen defiance.

Of course, it didn't work. At least, not in the way I expected. For finally, after all my frustration and anger and disillusionment was spent and I could hardly talk anymore from the hoarseness in my voice, I fell into a quiet whisper. I whispered for hours. I shared things with God I'd never said before—brutally honest things, things I'd never admitted even to myself.

And somewhere in the hushed confession of my exhausted heart, God showed up and loved me. In that moment of clarity, I realized that it wasn't my bravado, my anger, or even my desperate sincerity that allowed me to experience a deep connection with God that night. It was what came after all that—the honest, unfiltered, uncensored confession of my heart before God.

MAKE IT REAL!

When was the last time you honestly poured out your heart to God? In your journal, make a list of all the things you would talk about with God if you could spend just one hour in heaven with Jesus. Then set aside some time this week to honestly bring all of those issues before him.

WAITING TO EXHALE
Week 22—Thursday

My soul, wait in silence for God only, for my hope is from Him.
He only is my rock and my salvation, my stronghold; I shall not
be shaken. On God my salvation and my glory rest; the rock of
my strength, my refuge is in God. Trust in Him at all times, O
people; pour out your heart before Him; God is a refuge for us.
(Psalm 62:5-8, NASB)

WHAT does it mean to wait in silence for God? The waiting
that scripture so often promotes is nothing like the sort of waiting
we do in everyday life. It's not like waiting for a bus or waiting
for your food in a restaurant. It's nothing like waiting in line at
the bank or waiting for your car to be fixed. Waiting for God is at
once active and still. It is both quiet and emotionally raw.
Waiting on God is like standing on a stage before a crowd of
thousands with the spotlights in your eyes so you can't see a soul,
but you know they're there and you're waiting to see whether
they will respond to your voice. Waiting on God is like waiting to
exhale. The longer the waiting goes, the more desperate the need,
the more focused your desire, the more you see that his
appearance is the only thing in the universe that can bring you
genuine relief and give you life. Waiting like that is not a passive
thing at all. All of your attention is on him. Everything else pales
in comparison to your longing to connect—to hear from him, to
see him as he is, to follow him in everything.

This sort of waiting does not come easily to any of us.
Honestly, we are too busy for it; our lives, too frenetic. We are
distracted by worries and tasks that exist on the surface of our
thoughts—paying bills, meeting deadlines, pleasing people,
buying clothes that actually fit, watching our favorite shows, and
the like. Who has time to wait for God?

Typically, we enter into such seasons of waiting only when
life gets desperate. We've turned everywhere we can, and have
found no help, so we finally turn to God. Perhaps we scream at
him in anger and frustration for a while, enraged by the injustice
of our lot. But when that finally passes, we are left with nothing

but who we really are, and who he really is, and the space between us. It's only in such moments of raw honesty that powerful alliances are forged between his heart and ours.

MAKE IT REAL!

What is the space between you and God like these days? This week, spend an hour or two in silence before God. No music, no television or books or anything that might distract. Just stand in silence before him, and notice what is (or isn't) present in your connection with his Spirit. Write down your observations, then ask yourself, "What does this experience tell me about the level of connection and honesty in my relationship with God?"

CHOOSING HUMILITY
Week 22—Friday

O Lord, my heart is not proud, nor my eyes haughty;
nor do I involve myself in great matters, or in things too difficult
for me. Surely I have composed and quieted my soul; like a
weaned child rests against his mother, my soul is like a weaned
child within me.
(Psalm 131:1-2, NASB)

AT first glance, having an honest, open-hearted conversation with God sounds easy. Just tell him what you really think, right? Just tell him the truth of how you feel. But the truth we most need to share with him is often veiled even from us. It gets hidden away behind our pride, behind our fear of being exposed in the full light of day. When was the last time you took a long look at your own naked body in a full length mirror? For most of us, it's not a comfortable idea. Honest prayer is like that. You cannot hope to show God who you really are if you aren't also willing to see if for yourself.

   Humility is the only antidote for the pride that makes us hide—both from God and ourselves. What is the thing you are most ashamed to talk about with anyone? What is the deep truth about your life that you spend a lot of energy trying to ignore? That is where you must begin—first, by looking honestly and deeply at your own heart. What's really going on here? Don't shy away; take a good, long look. Then bring it all to God. Unvarnished. Uncensored. Honest. Show him what's there, and invite him to shine his light on all of it.

   Only that sort of humility will break the chains of shame, open the floodgates of God's grace and redemptive love, and ultimately, set you authentically free.

MAKE IT REAL!

Gather a handful of trusted friends together and discuss this question, "What is it to live in uncensored honesty before God?" Let everyone share his or her perspective (including you). Then spend time in prayer together, asking God to guide you all to his answer to the question.

WEEKEND REFLECTION

TAKE a few moments this weekend to review the devotions you've read over this past week, as well as the "Make It Real!" steps you've done. As you reflect on the week, get curious about how God is moving in and through your life. Use these questions as a guide:

- ❖ What insights have you gained over the past week?
- ❖ What changes or shifts are you noticing in your relationship with God? with others? with yourself?
- ❖ What "Make It Real!" steps were the most meaningful for you? What made them meaningful?
- ❖ How will you live differently next week as a result of what you've learned?
- ❖ What support do you need to help you make that change?
- ❖ Based on your experiences over the past week, what do you most need from God right now?
- ❖ What do you suppose God might be wanting most from you right now?

CHALLENGE: If you missed one of the "Make It Real!" steps for this week, set aside time this weekend to complete it, and record your reactions, insights, and results in your journal.

Be anxious for nothing, but in everything
by prayer and supplication with thanksgiving
let your requests be made known to God.
And the peace of God, which surpasses all comprehension,
will guard your hearts and your minds in Christ Jesus.
(Philippians 4:6-7, NASB)

THE end goal of an honest prayer life is not self-deprecation and self-judgment, but an entirely new kind of life. Those who choose humility and honest prayer no longer have anything to prove, or anything to hide—and that in itself is a beautiful way to live. But more than that, they are free from shame, for God's love has erased it. They can look at themselves honestly without flinching; they hold nothing back from God. They bring their failings, their needs, their wants and desires—all of it—to his throne every day. Entrusting it all to him, they take on his peace, which becomes for them a defensive weapon of war against the enemy's assault. They are not anxious.

This is not a wishful dream; rather, it is the authentic way of Christ—fully open and available to all who wish to follow him. All it takes is a sincere, authentic decision to humble yourself before God, to look honestly at yourself and bring all of that to him, and to wait before him until there is no longer need—as a servant waits upon her master (Psalm 123:2), as the watchman waits for the morning (Psalm 130:6).

MAKE IT REAL!

For a more in-depth journey into open-hearted prayer, consider asking a few friends to join you in reading one of the books listed in the "Book Study Group" list. Discuss the book together and spend time praying together to learn how praying with greater honesty and boldness impacts your faith.

BOOK STUDY GROUP
Daring to Draw Near by John White
Wrestling with God: Prayer That Never Gives Up by Greg Laurie
Getting Honest with God: Praying as if God Really Listens by
    Mark Littleton

Then he came there to a cave and lodged there; and behold, the
word of the Lord came to him, and He said to him,
"What are you doing here, Elijah?"
(1 Kings 19:9, NASB)

IMAGINE the scene: The great prophet Elijah has just been
threatened with death by Jezebel, the evil wife of King Ahab, and
Elijah knows very well that she has both the power and will to
make good on the threat. She wants him dead, and the sooner the
better. So the great prophet Elijah (who also happens to be just as
human as the rest of us) gets scared. Actually, he's terrified. And
so he scampers off to the wilderness to live in a cave, and
promptly starts pouting in anger at God for allowing him to be
put in such a precarious position. "I've been very zealous for
you," he complains to God, "I've done just as you asked; I've
carefully followed your ways. But you haven't come through for
me. This is not the life I signed up for. So I'm checking out. I'd
rather live in this cave than face what waits for me out there."

But God doesn't buy into Elijah's complaint. Instead, he says,
"'Go forth and stand on the mountain before the Lord.' And
behold, the Lord was passing by! And a great and strong wind
was rending the mountains and breaking in pieces the rocks
before the Lord; but the Lord was not in the wind. And after the
wind an earthquake, but the Lord was not in the earthquake. After
the earthquake a fire, but the Lord was not in the fire; and after
the fire a sound of a gentle blowing" (1 Kings 19:11-12). And
once God had revealed himself to Elijah, he asked again, "Now,
tell me, really this time: What are you doing here?"

For most people, life does not turn out the way we expect. We
expected to be married by now or at least in love—but we're not.
We expected our family relationships to be full of love and joy—
but they're not. We expected to be financial stable by now—but
we're not. We expected to know God's grand purpose for our
lives by now—but we don't. We expected to simply *feel happier*
by now than we actually do. And many of us have responded to

these disappointments the same way Elijah did—by running from the world and hiding out in caves of our own making.

So what about you? Are you one of those who have run away from a life that isn't what you hoped for? If so, what sort of cave have you crafted for yourself? And what are you doing there?

God's answer for Elijah was not to solve all his problems or answer all of his complaints. Rather, it was to pull back the veil, and offer Elijah a greater revelation of the majesty and glory and beauty and power and grace and holiness of who God is. Because, in the end, the courage it takes to leave your cave can come in no other way.

MAKE IT REAL!

In your journal, make a list of all the aspects of your life that have, so far, not turned out the way you hoped. Read back through the list once it is complete. Then journal your responses to these questions: How have these disappointments impacted the way you engage with your life? Where are you hiding from life? Where have you put your life on hold, waiting for some circumstance to change before you move forward? Where are you selling yourself (and your life) short because of disappointment over how things have turned out so far?

THE ONE PEARL
Week 23—Wednesday

The kingdom of heaven is like a treasure hidden in the field,
which a man found and hid again; and from joy over it
he goes and sells all that he has and buys that field.
Again, the kingdom of heaven is like a merchant seeking
fine pearls, and upon finding one pearl of great value,
he went and sold all that he had and bought it.
(Matthew 13:44-46, NASB)

TOO often we view God and our relationship with him as just one treasure among many that we desire. Certainly, we want God. And the life he wants for us—we want that too. But we also want many other things as well. We want to fall in love and get married. We want a family. We want financial freedom. We want the loft in the city or the home in the suburbs. We want health. We want fun and leisure. We want to be comfortable. We want to feel safe. The problem is not that we want all these things—such desires are all part of what it means to be human and should never be despised. The problem comes when our desire for these things rises to compete with our desire for God and his will for our lives.

Of all the followers of Christ in the world, it is arguably we in the West who are most prone to put our life for God on hold because of some lesser desire or another in our lives that has not yet been met. We live life on the sidelines, in the cold dank waiting room of the world—waiting for romance, waiting for financial success, waiting for God knows what. And all the while, God is waiting for us to wake up and realize that the rich, full life he offers us is not dependent on whether or not you get married, or get rich, or find success in your chosen career. His abundant gift of life is not locked away in the future of your dreams, but is right here, and right now.

"What are you doing here, Elijah?"

This is your life—today, right now. It may not be what you expected. You may not yet have all that you desire. But with Christ on the undisputed throne of your life, you already have living within you the makings of rich, courageous and a stunningly beautiful life. And the only one who can stop you from living it…is you.

<hr>
MAKE IT REAL!
<hr>

This week, grab some coffee with a couple of close friends and talk about your unmet desires in life. Share with them how any of your unmet desires have caused you to shrink back from living fully in favor of "waiting" until something in your circumstances changes. Ask them to pray with you for the grace and courage to stop waiting for life to happen, and go after all the richness and fullness that life with God offers right here, right now.

<hr>

Peter began to say to Him, "Behold, we have left everything and followed you." Jesus said, "Truly I say to you, there is no one who has left house or brothers or sisters or mother or father or children or farms, for My sake and for the gospel's sake, but that he will receive a hundred times as much now in the present age, houses and brothers and sisters and mothers and children and farms, along with persecutions; and in the age to come, eternal life. But many who are first will be last, and the last, first."
(Mark 10:28-31)

FOLLOWING the way of Christ is extraordinarily costly. It will cost you your right to your own way. It will require you to let go of your preconceived expectations of what your life should look like, as well as your right to any "thing"—such as wealth or poverty or marriage or singleness or family or health or comfort—that you think it must include. It will demand that you forfeit living out of your fear, and fully embrace the boldness and courage that comes from faith. The truth is, to follow him authentically will cost you everything. Anyone who tells you otherwise is lying to you.

But there is another side to the story. For the way of Christ is the grandest of adventures; it is an epic journey of personal and world transformation; it is the one, true path to experiencing an ever-deepening love relationship with your Creator, and through him, discovering the person you were always intended to be. The way of Christ is the most authentic and whole expression of Life possible on earth. And it opens the door to an eternity of life unending beyond your wildest imaginings.

So is it worth the cost?

As each new season of your life comes upon you, you must confront the question anew and answer it one way or the other. Perhaps it is a season of poverty or a season of singleness. Perhaps it is a season of obscurity or of betrayal. You do not know when the season will end, or really, if it ever will. Right there, in that place, the question is upon you. Will you shrink back, will you stop living fully, will you run to a cave and try to wait it out? Or will you follow him and boldly live your life to the full—right here, right now, right in the middle of this season of cost?

MAKE IT REAL!

What cost for following Christ are you not willing to pay? We all have such limits to our devotion, hidden away in our hearts. But you will not move beyond them until you first pull them into the light and name them for what they are. In your journal, list them out and share them with God. What is the thing that you cannot surrender to God for the sake of his call on your life?

*But whatever things were gain to me, those things I have counted
as loss for the sake of Christ. More than that, I count all things to
be loss in view of the surpassing value of knowing Christ Jesus
my Lord, for whom I have suffered the loss of all things, and
count them but rubbish so that I may gain Christ.*
(Philippians 3:7-8, NASB)

THE ultimate payoff for following the way of Christ is Christ
himself. As Paul declared, those who follow him willingly suffer
the loss of all things in order to gain him. Asaph likewise
declared in the Psalms, "Whom have I in heaven but You? And
besides You, I desire nothing on earth. My flesh and my heart
may fail, but God is the strength of my heart and my portion
forever" (Psalm 73:25-26).

But who is Christ that he would be worth losing everything
just to gain *him?*

It is a question worth considering, for it seems that most
Christians in the West don't believe he really is worth everything.
He is an add-on to their lives; a convenient philosophy, and a
talisman of good fortune. How could they know how great he is?
They haven't really tasted him. For once you do, you are ruined
for anything less than him and his purpose in your life. There is
no turning back. You may still suffer loss, but in the end it does
not matter any more that life has not turned out the way you
hoped or planned at first. For now you know the secret that the
world is dying to hear…that *he* is Life.

All next week, take time each morning to meditate on and pray through the portion of the "Daily Prayer for Freedom" provided at the end of this entry. The prayer was written by John Eldredge and is excerpted from his book, *Waking the Dead*.

If you'd like a complete copy of the prayer, visit www.ransomedheart.com to purchase the book. As you go through the week, notice how God responds to your sincere, authentic prayer to live your life wholly for him.

DAILY PRAYER FOR FREEDOM

"Dear God, holy and victorious Trinity, you alone are worthy of all my worship, my heart's devotion, all my praise and all my trust and all the glory of my life. I worship you, bow to you, and give myself over to you in my heart's search for life. You alone are Life, and you have become my life. I renounce all other gods, all idols, and I give you the place in my heart and in my life that you truly deserve. I confess here and now that it is all about you, God, and not about me. You are the Hero of this story, and I belong to you."

TAKE a few moments this weekend to review the devotions you've read over this past week, as well as the "Make It Real!" steps you've done. As you reflect on the week, get curious about how God is moving in and through your life. Use these questions as a guide:

- ❖ What insights have you gained over the past week?
- ❖ What changes or shifts are you noticing in your relationship with God? with others? with yourself?
- ❖ What "Make It Real!" steps were the most meaningful for you? What made them meaningful?
- ❖ How will you live differently next week as a result of what you've learned?
- ❖ What support do you need to help you make that change?
- ❖ Based on your experiences over the past week, what do you most need from God right now?
- ❖ What do you suppose God might be wanting most from you right now?

CHALLENGE: If you missed one of the "Make It Real!" steps for this week, set aside time this weekend to complete it, and record your reactions, insights, and results in your journal.

THE STEWARDSHIP OF YOUR LIFE
Week 24—Monday

And He directed the people to sit down on the ground; and taking
the seven loaves, He gave thanks and broke them, and started
giving them to His disciples to serve to them, and they served
them to the people.
(Mark 8:6, NASB)

ONCE we say yes to the call to follow Jesus, it isn't long before
we discover two life-shaking realities about him. First, that Jesus
really does love the world. He loves the beautiful and the ugly,
the glorious and the shattered, the convenient and the irritating
with equally infinite passion. He loves it all. He loves *them* all.

We think we know this about him from the beginning, of
course, but at the early stages of faith our understanding of the
love of God is a largely superficial thing, founded on little more
than a personal experience and an intellectual nod to the stories
we've heard about him. But as his heart settles within our own,
our spirits gradually awaken to the inescapable gravity and depth
of that love we thought we had already studied and defined, and
we quickly bow to the truth that we don't understand it at all—for
it is too vast, too deep and too strong for our minds to
comprehend.

Instead, our knowledge of his love begins to come from a
place deeper than intellect or even than faith. We come to know
his love for the world as a man's lungs know air. We know it by
breathing it in, by surrendering to its filling, and tasting it for
ourselves.

But he does not stop there. For no sooner do we taste the
unfathomable love of God than we are shocked with a second
revelation: He has chosen to share the gift of this immense love
for the world through us. That is, *through you.*

Today, he is handing you his love as simply as he handed the
loaves to his disciples on the mountainside, and is instructing you
to pass it on to the masses. The miracle is still his, for it is his
love you hold in your hands. But he has made you its steward,
and in doing so, he has done the unthinkable: He has given you

the power to decide whether the gift of his love will reach the world or whither in your hands.

MAKE IT REAL!

How has God loved others through you this week? In your journal, list all the situations you can think of in which God was free to demonstrate love through you. What does your list tell you about the way God most often expresses himself through you? How could you become a better steward of his love in the weeks to come?

YOUR GIFT TO THE WORLD
Week 24—Tuesday

As each one has received a special gift, employ it in serving one
another as good stewards of the manifold grace of God.
(1 Peter 4:10, NASB)

THOUGH God's love is constant, its expression through each
of us is unique. I can never love the way you can love. I can
never bless another human soul in the unique way that you can. I
can never give to the world the gift that you can give—for the
gift that God entrusted to me is not like yours. Your gift, your
treasure, is as unique and priceless as you are.

What is the gift that God has put in you to give to the world?
What is the legacy he has called you to leave in your wake? This
is not a question about a degree plan or a career choice; it goes
far deeper than that. It has much more to do with *who you are*
than with what you do to pay the bills. As followers of Christ, we
are, each of us, unique expressions of God's love in the world.
We are each like Frodo in our way—bestowed with a unique
quest from God that we alone can fulfill. And just as Galadriel
said to the valiant hobbit, so God says to us, "If you do not find a
way, no one will."

We tend not to think this way, perhaps because it feels a little
heady and self-important to our religious sensibilities. We tend to
hold back in the safety of thinking that our gift is all God and
none of us. And if we do not find a way to fulfill our purpose and
give our gift fully to the world, we suspect that someone else will
step in to take up the slack. But if that were the case, God would
have made us all clones of one another.

You are God's unique steward, and the gift he has given you
to give away is more than simply your money or your time. It is
your deepest self—your love, your passion, your unique
expression of his gospel in the world. And if you do not find a
way to unleash that gift and release it to the world, no one will.

MAKE IT REAL!

What is the gift that God has put in you to give to the world? To help you find out, try this: Ask a few of your closest friends to tell you honestly what *they* think your gift to the world is. Then write out your own description of your gift, based on what they tell and your own impressions in the Spirit.

For you were called to freedom, brethren;
only do not turn your freedom into an opportunity for the flesh,
but through love serve one another.
(Galatians 5:13, NASB)

THERE are many passions that can motivate people to give
their gift fully to the world: greed, fame, fear, power, wealth, and
pride, to name a few. But for Christians, there is only one
motivation for greatness that God supports—and that is Love.
Perhaps that is why so few followers of Christ aspire to become
great givers and doers in the world, because so few of us
understand how deeply we are loved by God, and thus, how
powerful that love could be if we unleashed it through our lives.

   We are stewards of nothing less that the call of Christ
himself: "The Spirit of the Sovereign Lord is on me, because the
Lord has anointed me to preach good news to the poor. He has
sent me to bind up the brokenhearted, to proclaim freedom for the
captive, and release from darkness for the prisoners, to proclaim
the year of the Lord's favor..." (Isaiah 61:1-2a). Jesus has set us
free to love, and made us stewards of that all-powerful gift within
the world. How each of us expresses that gift is as varied and
unique as we are. But do not think for a second that because you
are not Mother Teresa or Billy Graham that you are not called to
greatness. For you are a steward of the same Christ they have
served. And the gifts he has given you are just as powerful and
needed in the world.

MAKE IT REAL!

If you could do anything you wanted for God, and knew that you
couldn't fail—what would you do? Write a detailed description
of your dream, and then show it to a few trusted Christian friends.
Ask them to join you in praying for God to show you the next
steps you can take this month to steward your dream toward
reality.

THE BATTLE OF STEWARDSHIP
Week 24—Thursday

...for a wide door for effective service has opened to me,
and there are many adversaries.
(1 Corinthians 16:9, NASB)

YOU cannot be an effective steward of the gifts God has placed in you unless you are willing to step into battle, and to stay in the battle as long as it takes to see your gifts released in their fullness. For there are many adversaries, both spiritual and natural, who will stand in your way, but they cannot stop you so long as you believe (1 John 5:4). The battle to which God has called you—the battle to steward the gifts, the talents, the heart God has given you—is fundamentally a battle of faith. But this is no faith of armchair theologians, or pew-sitting spectators. This is the faith of the real world, the faith of warriors, the faith that does not say "I hope," but rather proclaims "I know!"

The great follower of Christ, Dietrich Bonhoeffer, wrote, "Action springs not from thought, but from a readiness for responsibility." The call of stewardship that rests on you is a call to believe—but it is also a call to bold action. Are you ready to take responsibility for the treasure God has placed in you, and the gifts he has given you? Are you ready to step up and take your place in his kingdom, and fight for the full release of the gift that God has placed in you to give to the world?

You will know your answer not by your words, but by your actions.

MAKE IT REAL!

What is the "wide door of effective service" that you've been hesitating to step through? If you let go of your hesitation and took action this week—what's the first thing you would need to do? What's the second? And then what? Commit to taking those three steps over the next week, and see what happens.

THE BEGINNING OF THE JOURNEY
Week 24—Friday

For to me, to live is Christ and to die is gain.
(Philippians 1:21)

SOMEDAY soon we will pass through the final curtain from this world, and the deepest and truest part our life story will begin. We will be welcomed with an experience of joy, the likes of which have never seen or known on earth, by the glorious free who have gone before us. And we will see him—the One for Whom we have lived all these years—as we have never seen him before. Not dimly, as we do now, but with such stunning clarity and brilliance that we will wonder how we could have ever thought the sun was bright. And the sight of his laughter will in that instant unleash our hearts to soar and sing and laugh and dance and beautifully transform in the delight of our absolute redemption. All thought of the cost we have paid for his cause will be gone, swallowed up in the ecstasy of knowing that he truly is, in every way, everything our hearts have ever longed for since we first drew breath.

Whatever gifts he may grant us, we will cast at his feet. For we will know; we will finally know that we have won the race. We have been won by him. And we will dance before his throne, just like David before the Ark—joyfully, in wild abandon.

Each of us who follows Christ will experience that moment. And when you do, it will mark the beginning of life as only your deepest heart hoped it could be.

And so we have hope on our trek through this world, regardless of the struggles we must muddle through while we're here. And we cling to fierce courage and tenacity to stay in the race and complete the call of God's grace upon our lives. It is but a short time, after all. And we know that what follows after is by far the better journey.

MAKE IT REAL!

No one knows exactly what heaven will be like, but God has revealed something of its reality within your deepest heart (Ecclesiastes 3:11). This week, write a description of heaven as your heart most deeply longs for it to be. Place that description in your Bible and read it anytime you feel like giving up or falling short of God's call on your life in this world.

AN INVITATION TO HELP

IF you have been inspired by this book and its message, you may have already thought of some people you'd like to recommend it to. That's great—please do! In addition, here are some other ways we would really appreciate your help in spreading the word:

- ❖ If you have a website or blog, consider sharing a bit about the book and how it touched your life.
- ❖ Write a book review on Amazon.com.
- ❖ If you own a shop or business, consider buying some books to resell to your customers.
- ❖ If you know people who are in a position to promote the book to wider audience, buy them a copy and encourage them to consider promoting it to others.
- ❖ Go through the book together in your small group Bible study.
- ❖ Encourage your pastor to use the book as a discipleship tool in your faith community.
- ❖ Buy a set of books to donate to prisons, church bookstores, women's shelters—anywhere people might be encouraged by its message.
- ❖ Talk about the book on e-mail lists or online forums you belong to, or other online communities you frequent.

Thanks! Word of mouth makes all the difference in helping a book like this gain visibility to a wider audience.

Printed in the United Kingdom by
Lightning Source UK Ltd., Milton Keynes
138325UK00002B/39/P